Level B

Lesley Mandel Morrow
Senior Author

Jane M. Carr | Emily A. Faubion | Joanne M. McCarty

Margaret M. McCullough | Lisa P. Piccinino | Diane M. Richner | Patricia Scanlon

Monica T. Sicilia | Geraldine M. Timlin | Anne F. Windle

Program Consultants

Grace R. Cavanagh, Ed.D.
Principal, P.S. 176
Board of Education
New York, New York

Melanie R. Kuhn, Ph.D.
Assistant Professor of Literacy
Rutgers University
New Brunswick, New Jersey

Sharon L. Suskin, M.A.
Assessment Specialist
South Brunswick Public Schools
South Brunswick, New Jersey

Ann S. Wright
Reading Consultant
Bridgeport Public Schools
Bridgeport, Connecticut

Maggie Pagan, Ed.S.
College of Education, ESOL Specialist
University of Central Florida
Orlando, Florida

Donna A. Shadle
Principal
St. Mary Elementary and Preschool
Massillon, Ohio

Maria T. Driend
Reading Consultant
Cooperative Educational Services
Trumbull, Connecticut

Eleanor M. Vargas, M.A.
Resource Specialist Teacher
Los Angeles Unified School District
Los Angeles, California

Helen Wood Turner, Ed.D.
Deputy Director of Education
Associates for Renewal in Education
Washington, D.C.

Eydee Schultz
Staff Development Specialist
Independent Consultant
Springfield, Illinois

Frances E. Horton
Supervisor, Title I
Cabell County Public Schools
Huntington, West Virginia

Deborah A. Scigliano, Ed.D.
First Grade Teacher
Assumption School
Pittsburgh, Pennsylvania

Sadlier-Oxford
A Division of William H. Sadlier, Inc.

Advisors

The publisher wishes to thank the following teachers and administrators who read portions of the series prior to publication for their comments and suggestions.

Margarite K. Beniaris
Assistant Principal
Chicago, Illinois

Kathleen Cleary
First Grade Teacher
Warminster, PA

Noelle Deinken
Kindergarten Teacher
Thousand Oaks, California

Susan Dunlap
Second Grade Teacher
Noblesville, Indiana

Jean Feldman
Consultant, NCEE
Brooklyn, New York

Deborah Gangstad
First Grade Teacher
Carmel, Indiana

Angela Gaudioso
First Grade Teacher
Brooklyn, New York

Sr. Dawn Gear, G.N.S.H.
Principal
Atlanta, Georgia

Mary Lee Gedwill
Second Grade Teacher
North Ridgeville, Ohio

Ana Gomez
Second Grade Teacher
Kenner, Louisiana

Patricia McNamee
Principal
Orlando, Florida

Laura A. Holzheimer
L.A. Resource Teacher, Title I
Cleveland, Ohio

Sr. Paul Mary Janssens, O.P.
Principal
Springfield, Illinois

Stephanie Wilson
Second Grade Teacher
Knightstown, Indiana

Melissa Mannetta
First Grade Teacher
Brooklyn, New York

Adelaide Hanna
Reading Resource Teacher
Brooklyn, New York

Sr. Francis Helen Murphy, I.H.M.
Editorial Advisor
Philadelphia, Pennsylvania

JoAnn C. Nurdjaja
Staff Developer
Brooklyn, New York

Mary Jo Pierantozzi
Educational Consultant
Philadelphia, Pennsylvania

Antoinette Plewa
Principal
North Plainfield, New Jersey

Pedro Rodriguez
First Grade Teacher
Los Angeles, California

Dawn M. Trocchio
Kindergarten Teacher
Brooklyn, New York

Rosemarie Valente
Second Grade Teacher
Newark, New Jersey

Earl T. Wiggins
Program Specialist, Title I
Lehigh, Florida

Acknowledgments

Special thanks to Sr. Irene Loretta, IHM, for her advice and counsel during the early developmental stages of the *Sadlier Phonics* program.

Every good faith effort has been made to locate the owners of copyrighted material to arrange permissions to reprint selections.

William H. Sadlier, Inc., gratefully acknowledges the following for the use of copyrighted materials:

"A Friend" (text only) by Betsy Jones Michael. Reprinted by permission of the author.

"Trees" (text only) by Harry Behn is the full text of TREES by Harry Behn (A Bill Martin Book published by Henry Holt) Copyright 1949 Harry Behn. © Renewed 1977 Alice L. Behn. Used by permission of Marian Reiner.

"City Street" (text only) by Lois Lenski from WE LIVE IN THE CITY, © 1954 by Lois Lenski. Reprinted by permission of The Lois Lenski Covey Foundation.

"The Museum Door" (text only) by Lee Bennett Hopkins. Reprinted by permission of Curtis Brown, Ltd. Copyright © 1973 by Lee Bennett Hopkins. Also appears in DINOSAURS, published by Harcourt, Brace, Jovanovich, 1987.

"What Is Brown?" (text only) from HAILSTONES AND HALIBUT BONES by Mary O'Neill and Leonard Weisgard, Ill. Copyright © 1961 by Mary LeDuc O'Neill. Used by permission of Doubleday, a division of Bantam Doubleday Dell Publishing Group, Inc.

ZB Font Method Copyright © 1996 Zaner-Bloser

Product Development and Management

Leslie A. Baranowski

Photo Credits

Neal Farris: Cover

Eakal Ali: 102 background, 102b. Animals Animals/Earth Scenes—Richard Shiell: 147 *top.* Jane Bernard: 225b. Cate Photography: 184, 225, 226. Corbis/Tim Thompson: 102a; E. R. Degginger: 147 *bottom center;* The Art Institute of Chicago/photograph ©1995, All rights reserved: 107 *left.* Neal Farris: 41, 77, 101, 137, 159, 160, 185, 187, 21. Garden Image/Peter Symcox: 163 Gerald Tang: 163. Valerie Henschel: 228 *bottom right.* Hutchings Photography: 188. Image Bank/G.K. & Vikki Hart: 176. Ken Karp: 15 *bottom, 78.* Kohout Productions/Root Resources: 147 *top right.* Viesti Associates/R. Pasley: 105 *right.* Greg Lord: 42, 60, 102c, 138, 168, 218. The Picture Cube/D. & I. MacDonald: 227 *bottom left;* John Coletti: 235 *top right;* Emily Stone: 239 *top right;* Stanley Rown: 240 *left.* H. Armstrong Roberts: 41 *right,* 163 *bottom right,* 220 *bottom left.* Kevin Schafer: 227 *bottom right,* 228 *bottom left,* 236 *top left.* Ellis Nature Photo/Jeremy Stafford-Deitsch: 235 *bottom left.* The Stock Market/Lew Long: 15 *top right;* Roy Morsch: 15 *center right;* ChromoSohm: 81 *left;* Kunio Owaki: 141 *right;* R. Berenholtz: 141 *left;* Thomas Braise: 239 *top left.* Photodisc: 191e. Photonica/Fumio Oi: 191 background; Plastock: 191b, 191d, 191g. SUPERSTOCK: 236 *bottom right.* FPG International/Thayer Syme: 235 *top left.* Stone/Vincent Oliver: 124a; Ian Murphy: 15 *top left;* David Hiser: 15 *center left;* Doug Armand: 45 *background,* 239 *background;* Suzanne & Nick Geary: 45 *right;* Joe Ortner: 105 *center right;* Doris DeWitt: 105 *center left;* Hugh Sitton: 105 *left;* Hideo Kurihara: 221 *top left;* Bert Sagara: 221 *top right;* Rainer Grosskopf: 221 *bottom;* Terry Vine: 227 *top left;* Peter Timmermans: 228 *top left;* Jeanne Drake: 235 *bottom right;* Chip Henderson: 240 *right.* Mark Turner: 236 *top right.* Larry Ulrich Photography: 227 *top right,* 228 *top right.*

Illustrators

Dirk Wunderlich: Cover

Bernard Adnet: 34, 131, 233, 234; JoLynn Alcorn: 150; David Bergstein: 57, 157, 198; David Brion: 87; Jenny Campbell: 37, 55, 83, 95; Nancy Carpenter: 5; Peter Church: 143; Kathy Couri: 31; Hector Cuenca: 42; David Edgington: 59; Rusty Fletcher: 22, 54, 71, 121, 153, 204, 209; Laura Freeman: 38, 179, 218; Arthur Friedman: 43, 44, 110, 126; Dave Garbot: 50, 85, 113; Patrick Girouard: 147, 203; Adam Gordon: 60, 239, 240; Tom Graham: 20; Peter Grosshauser: 49, 73, 109, 133; Myron Grossman: 139, 140, 158; Tim Haggerty: 11, 67, 91, 93, 112, 181, 213, 231, 232; Melanie Hall: 52; Laurie Hamilton: 88, 136; Joan Holub: 26; Jui Ishida: 115, 119; Nathan Jarvis: 7, 27, 97, 123, 124, 129, 165, 188; Megan Jeffrey: 98; Chris Lensch: 23; Andy Levine: 32, 51, 56, 61, 62 69, 72, 111, 132, 155, 181, 197; Jason Levinson: 28, 65; Tammie Lyon: 35, 154, 167, 175, 180; Maria Pia Marrella: 78, 138, 160; Cheryl Mendenhall: 74, 146; Patrick Merrill: 63, 107; Albert Molnar: 53, 122, 145; John Nez: 75, 79, 80; Michele Noiset: 193; Iva O'Conner: 130; Olivia: 161, 162, 171, 172; Chris Reed: 33; Mick Reid: 149; Bart Rivers: 19; Lizzy Rockwell: 64; Veronica Rooney: 58; Cindy Rosenheim: 30; BB Sams: 9; Roz Schanzer: 10, 21, 25, 89, 103, 104, 212; Jamie Smith: 116; Theresa Smith: 47; Jackie Snider: 195, 211; Sally Springer: 13, 29, 86; Daryl Stevens: 121, 135, 170, 189, 190; Steve Sullivan: 6, 18, 48, 84, 108, 114, 144, 166, 194; Don Tate: 120, 148, 179, 207; Erin Terry: 134; Sally Vitsky: 17, 70; Vicki Wehrman: 229, 230; Susan Williams: 219, 220; Toby Williams: 237, 238. Functional Art: Diane Ali, Sommer Keller, and Michael Woo.

Address inquiries to Permissions Department, William H. Sadlier, Inc., 9 Pine Street, New York, New York 10005-1002.

S is a registered trademark of William H. Sadlier, Inc.

Printed in the United States of America.

ISBN: 0-8215-7002-1
456789/04 03

Contents

1 Initial, Final, and Medial Consonants

2 Short Vowels

3 Long Vowels

4 Variant Consonant Sounds and Consonant Blends

5 Syllables, Compound Words, y as a Vowel, Consonant Digraphs, and r-controlled Vowels

6 Vowel Digraphs and Diphthongs

7 Contractions, Plurals, and Inflectional Endings

8 Suffixes, Prefixes, Synonyms, Antonyms, and Homonyms

Read Aloud

A Friend

It's fun to have a friend!
Someone to see and stay with
To walk and talk and play with
To laugh and shout HURRAY with
It's fun to have a friend!

We might not even talk!
We might just sit and giggle
Until we wiggle-wiggle
Or leap and jump and jiggle
We might not even talk!

It's fun to have a friend!
To hold a hand and go with
To ask and learn and know with
To sing and dance and grow with
It's fun to have a friend!

Betsy Jones Michael

Critical Thinking

Why is it fun to have a friend?
How can you make new friends?

Name ______________________________

Dear Family,

As your child progresses through this unit about friendship, he or she will review the sounds of the consonants. The 21 letters of the alphabet that are consonants are shown below.

- Point to each consonant and have your child say its name.

Apreciada Familia:

En esta unidad, acerca de la amistad, su niño repasará los sonidos de las consonantes. Las siguientes letras son las 21 consonantes del idioma inglés.

- Señale cada consonante y pida al niño decir el nombre.

- Read the poem "A Friend" on the reverse side. Talk about things friends do together.
- Read the poem again. Ask your child to say the first and last lines of each stanza with you.
- Help your child identify some of the consonants in the poem. Ask what sounds they make.

- Lea al niño la poesía "A Friend" en la página 5. Converse con su niño acerca de lo que hacen los amigos cuando están juntos.
- Lea el poema de nuevo. Pida a su hijo recitar con usted los dos primeros versos de cada estrofa.
- Repasen las consonantes que aparecen en la poesía. ¿Cómo suenan?

PROJECT

Ask your child to name some of his or her friends. Together, make a list of the names. Underline single consonants in each name. Then have your child choose one friend and write, call, or draw him or her.

PROYECTO

Pida a su niño nombrar a algunos de sus amigos. Después escriban los nombres. Subrayen las consonantes en cada nombre. Luego pídale escribir una carta, llamar, o dibujar a uno de los amigos.

Name ______________________________

Pals begins with the sound of **p.** Listen for beginning consonant sounds in the rhyme.

We're best pals,
So meet me at noon
To take a fun ride
In a hot-air balloon.

The letters **b, c, d, f, g, h, j, k, l, m, n, p, q, r, s, t, v, w, x, y,** and **z** are consonants.

Say the name of each picture. Write the letter or letters that stand for the beginning consonant sound.

j	m	k	f	z	s	r	b	qu	h	w	p

1	2	3	4
5	6	7	8
9	10	11	12

Say the name of each picture. Write the letter that stands for the beginning consonant sound.

1 ___og	2 ___et	3 ___ug	4 10 ___en
5 ___ite	6 ___an	7 ___ig	8 ___ase
9 ___arn	10 ___ake	11 ___at	12 SUGARLESS ___um
13 ___un	14 ___ap	15 ___ut	16 ___op

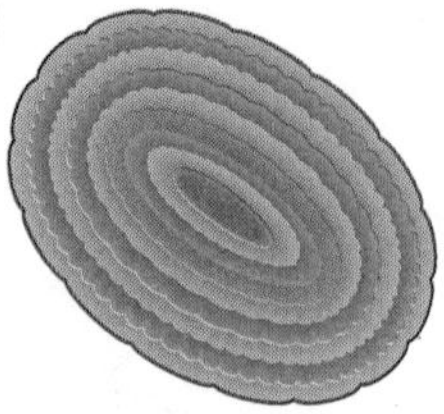

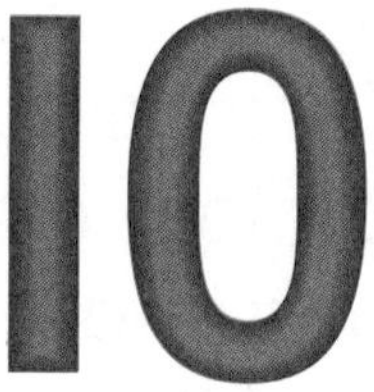

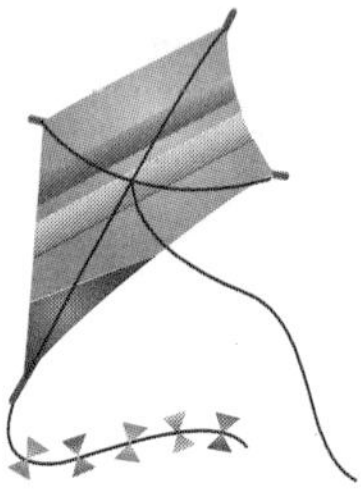

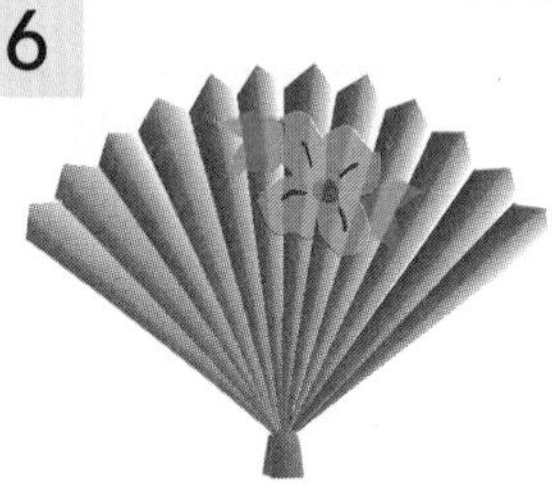

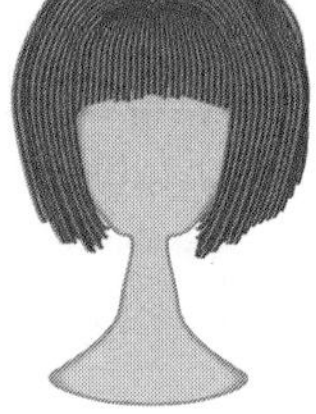

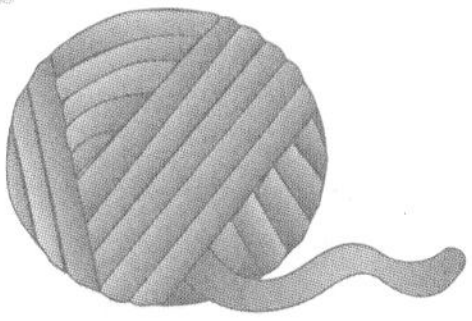

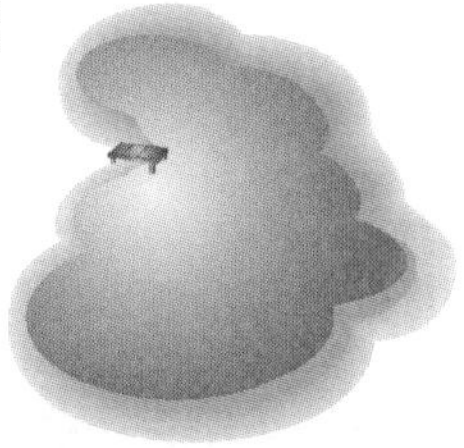

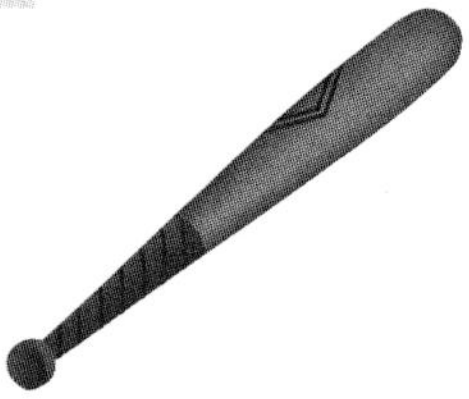

LESSON 2: Connecting Sound to Symbol: Initial Consonants

Ask your child to say another word that begins with the same consonant sound as each picture name.

Name ______________________________

Great ends with the sound of **t**. Listen for ending consonant sounds in the rhyme.

You're great. You're fun.
I like you, bud.
I like you better
Than a pig likes mud.

Say the name of each picture. Circle the letter or letters that stand for the ending consonant sound.

1 b d t	2 p m g	3 l b g
4 ff ss ll	5 l m j	6 t d n
7 k h f	8 m c n	9 zz tt dd
10 tt gg zz	11 h s n	12 w f k
13 d f k	14 t x d	15 ff ll dd

Say the name of each picture. Write the letter that stands for the ending consonant sound.

1	2	3	4
cu	boo	te	be
5	**6**	**7**	**8**
fo	tai	ga	ha
9	**10**	**11**	**12**
gu	ca	lea	bu
13	**14**	**15**	**16**
li	po	ne	fa

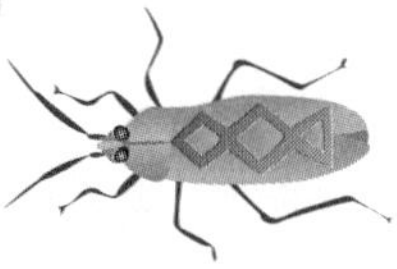

Change the **t** in **hat** to **d.** Write the new word. Use the word in a sentence.

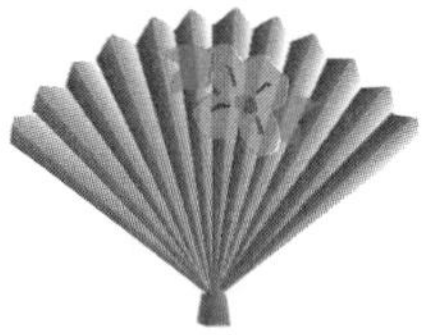

LESSON 3: Connecting Sound to Symbol: Final Consonants

Name the letters of the alphabet with your child. Take turns saying words that end with each consonant.

Name ______________________________

Shadow has the sound of **d** in the middle. Listen for middle consonant sounds in the rhyme.

My buddy Shadow
Follows me all day.
But when the sunny day is gone,
She cannot stay and play.

Say the name of each picture. Draw a line from the picture to the letter or letters that stand for the middle consonant sound.

1		**v**	7		**ll**
2	7	**m**	8		**tt**
3		**b**	9		**g**
4	1 2 3 4 5 6 7 8 9 10 11 12	**c**	10		**n**
5		**t**	11		**pp**
6		**l**	12		**mm**

Say the name of each picture. Write the letter that stands for the middle consonant sound.

1	2	3
le on	sa ad	ro in

4	5	6
wa er	se en	ca el

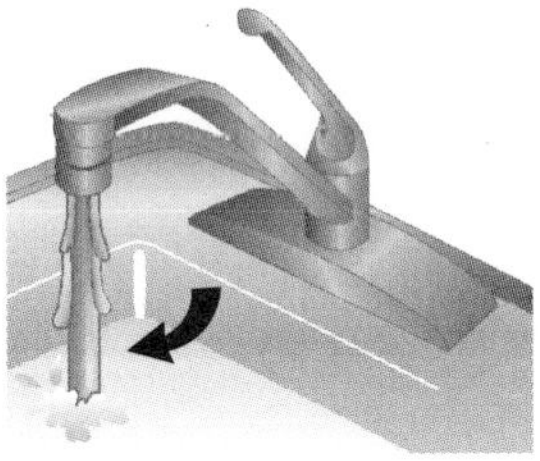

7	8	9
ca in	tu ip	ti er

10	11	12
ro ot	dra on	spi er

LESSON 4: Connecting Sound to Symbol: Medial Consonants

PHONICS Alive at Home

Which three pictures have the same middle consonant sound in their names? Have your child find them.

Name ____

Look at the picture clues. Fill in the missing letters in the puzzles.

ACROSS

4 7

5

6

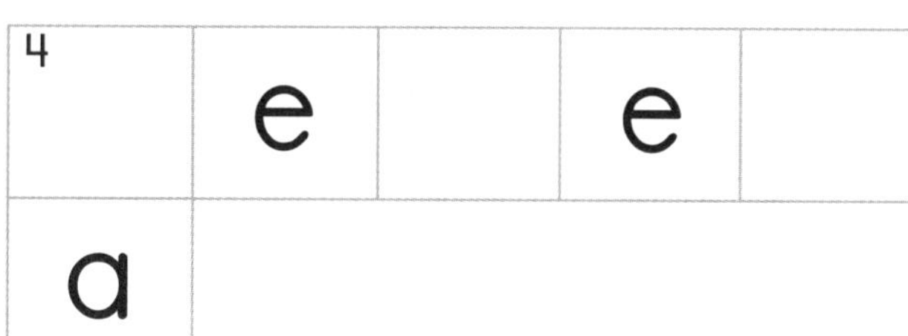

DOWN

4

a

6 o

What seven things would you and your friend put in a backpack? Name each thing and write the letters that stand for the beginning and ending consonant sounds.

Write the missing letter in each picture name. Then find a rhyming word in the box and write it on the line below.

foxes	hat	hop	mug	pedal	pen	pig	van

1 _at

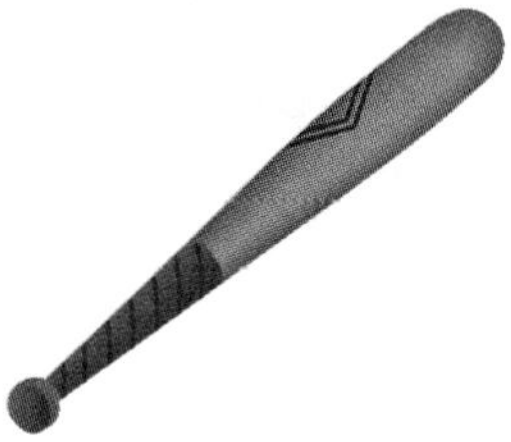

2 bo_es

3 wi_

4 _en

5 me_al

6 ca_

7 _ug

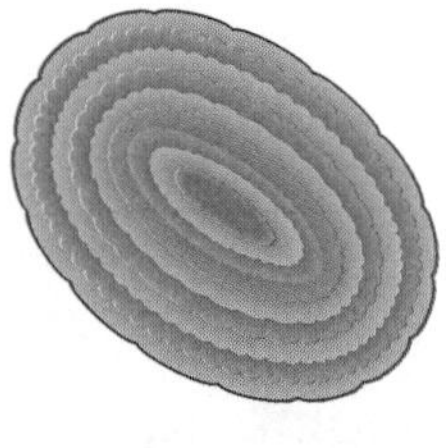

8 po_

PHONICS Alive at Home

Ask your child to name the letters he or she wrote to complete the picture names.

Name ______________________________

Look and Learn

Let's read and talk about friendship.

We're best **buddies** in English.
In Spanish, we're **amigos.**
Speak French and call us **amis.**
I'll speak Swahili and call you **rafiki.**
You speak Japanese and call
me **tomodachi.**
In any language, we're friends.

How are friends the same all over the world?

LESSON 6: Initial, Final, and Medial Consonants in Context
Comprehension: Making Generalizations

Say the name of each picture. Write the letter that stands for the missing sound.

1 og	2 am	3 arn
4 fo	5 10 te	6 hoo
7 sa ad	8 le on	9 ro ot
10 op	11 wa er	12 pi

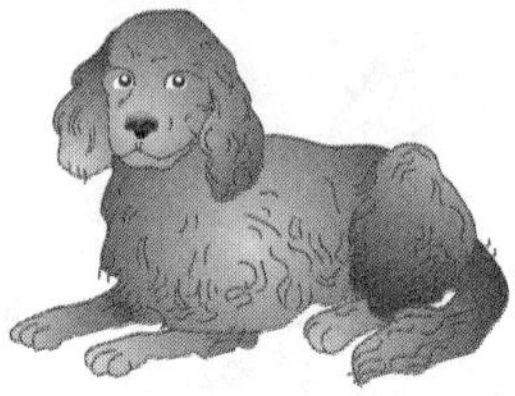

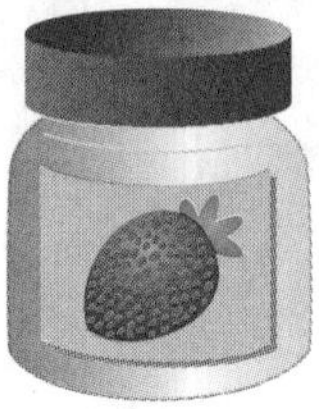

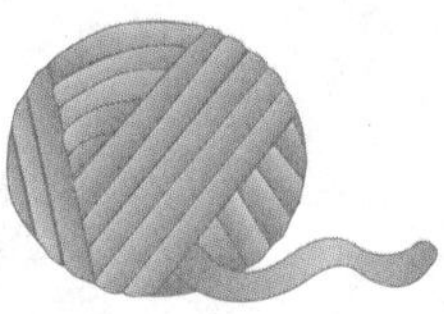

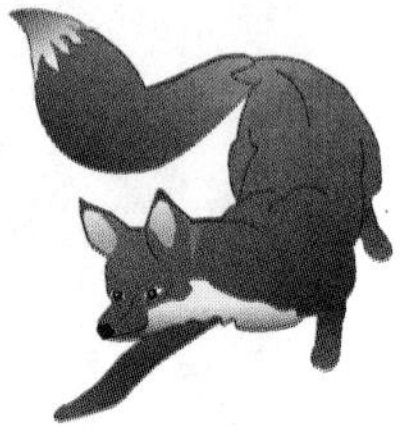

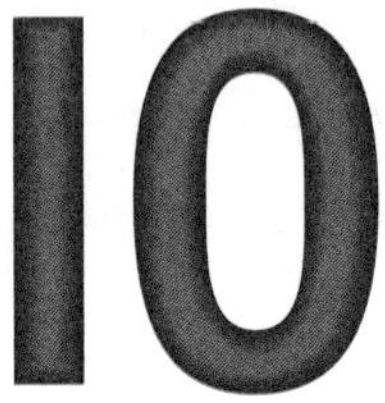

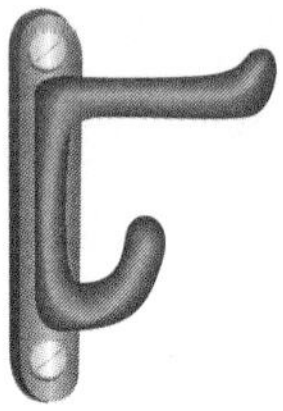

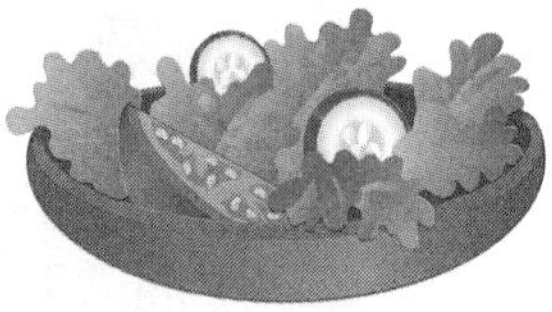

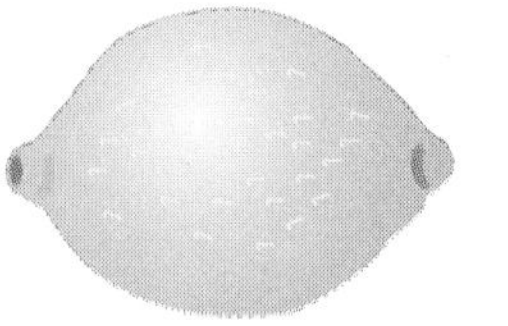

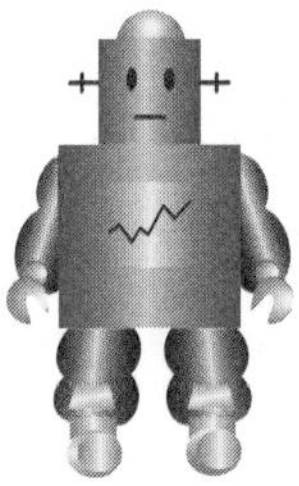

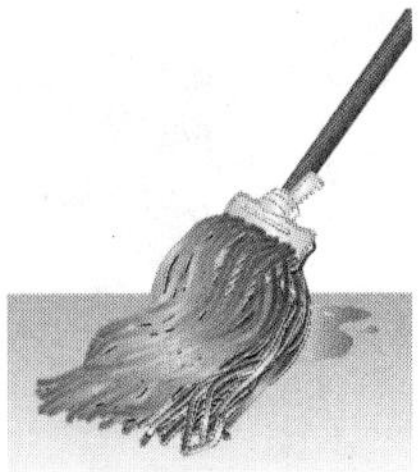

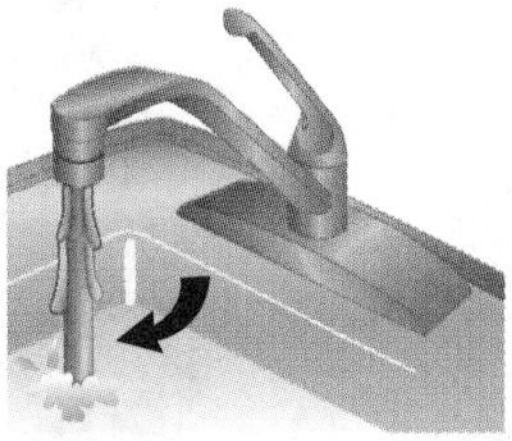

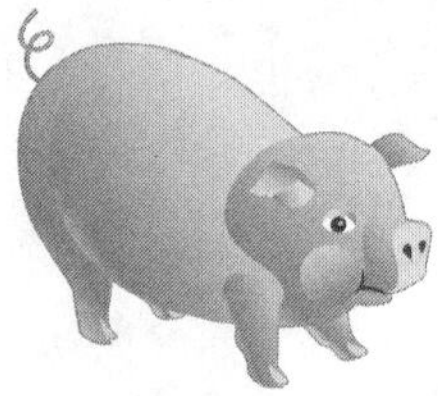

PHONICS Alive at Home Review this Check-Up with your child.

Read Aloud

SAMPAN

Waves lap lap
Fish fins clap clap
Brown sails flap flap
Chop-sticks tap tap
Up and down the long green river
Ohe Ohe lanterns quiver
Willow branches brush the river
Ohe Ohe lanterns quiver
Waves lap lap
Fish fins clap clap
Brown sails flap flap
Chop-sticks tap tap

Tao Lang Pee

Critical Thinking

What sights might you see along a river?
What sounds might you hear?

Name ________________________________

Dear Family,

As your child progresses through this unit about water and rivers, she or he will review the short vowel sounds of **a**, **i**, **o**, **u**, and **e.**

- Say the picture names together and listen to the short vowel sound in the middle of each word.

Apreciada Familia:

En esta unidad, acerca del agua y los ríos, su niño repasará el sonido corto de las vocales **a, i, o, u, e.**

- Pronuncien el nombre de las cosas en los cuadros y escuchen el sonido corto de las vocales en cada palabra.

a	i	o	u	e
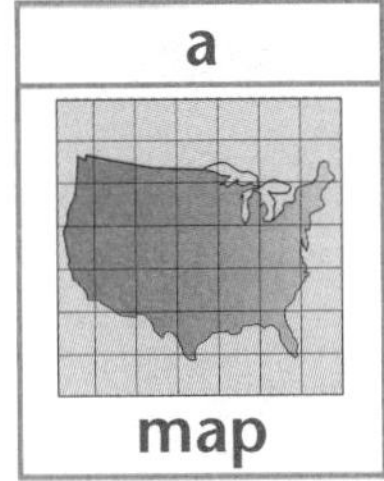		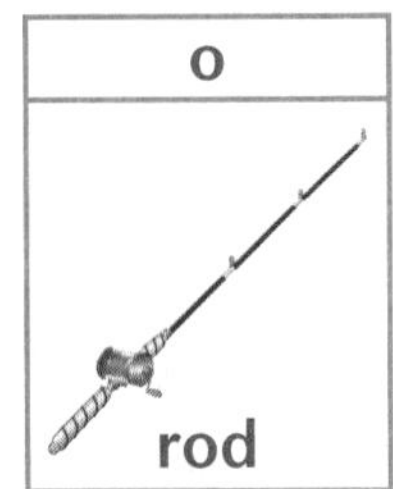		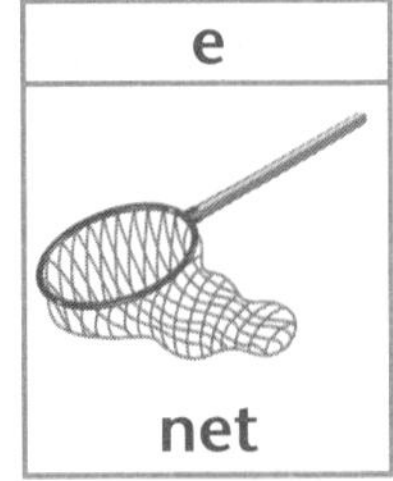
map	**fin**	**rod**	**tug**	**net**

- Read the poem "Sampan" on the reverse side. Talk about what it might be like to live on a boat.
- Read the poem again. Together, look for the rhyming words that sound like what they mean. **(lap lap, clap clap, flap flap, tap tap)**
- Help your child find short vowel words in the poem. **(lap, fish, fins, clap, flap, chop, sticks, tap, up, brush)**

- Lea a su niño "Sampan" en la página 17. Hablen sobre como sería vivir en un barco.
- Lea el poema de nuevo. Busquen las palabras que rimen y cuyo sonido se parezca a su significado. **(lap lap, clap clap, flap flap, tap tap)**
- Ayude al niño a encontrar palabras en la poesía donde el sonido de la vocal sea corto. **(lap, fish, fins, clap, flap, chop, sticks, tap, up, brush)**

PROJECT

On a large sheet of paper, draw a picture of a river. Cut out small pieces of paper in the shape of logs. When your child learns a new short vowel word, have him or her write the word on a log and tape it on the river.

PROYECTO

Dibuje un río en un papel grande. Corte pedacitos de papel en forma de tronco. Cuando el niño reconozca una palabra con vocales de sonido corto puede escribirla en un papelito y pegarla en el río.

Name ______________________________

Sat has the short **a** sound. Listen for the sound of short **a** in the rhyme.

Two crabs sat
In sandy mud flats,
With mud for their beds
And mud for their hats.

Helpful Hint

If a syllable or word has only one vowel and it comes at the beginning or between two consonants, the vowel usually has the **short** sound.

Circle and write the short **a** word that names each picture. In the last box, draw a picture for a short **a** word. Write the word.

1 mat map cat	2 fan tan fat	3 fad cap cab
4 gas sag gap	5 bag flat flag	6 yam jam ram
7 hand land sand	8 tax tag wax	9

Say the phonogram. Circle two pictures that have that phonogram in their names. Write the picture names.

1 _ag	2 _am	3 _an	4 _at
			WELCOME
25¢			

Write a silly sentence with two rhyming short **a** words. Tell what you can take on a raft. For example, "I can take a **ram** and a **ham.**"

Ask your child to name another short **a** word that rhymes with each pair of rhyming words.

Name ______________________________

Look at the picture. Circle and write the word that completes the sentence. Then read the sentences and have a partner name the short **a** words.

1	Dad and Sam ____________ lunch.	tack pack tap
2	They load the ____________.	van yam man
3	Dad stops for a ____________.	pan nap map
4	The map leads to the ____________.	lamp camp cap
5	Sam sees a ____________ beaver.	fad pal fat
6	It ____________ a flat tail.	pass hat has
7	It swims very ____________!	fast sat cast

Read the poem. Underline the short **a** words. Then use short **a** words to complete the sentences.

The Sand Band

Sam the Clam claps, claps, claps.
Pam the Crab cracks, cracks, cracks.
Tad the Turtle flaps, flaps, flaps.

That sand band plays
In sand and sun.
They play all day.
The friends have fun.

A wave comes by,
Slap, crash, WH-E-E-E,
And all the friends dance out to sea.

1. Sam the Clam ____________.

2. Pam cracks and Tad ____________.

3. The band plays in the ____________ and sun.

4. The friends ____________ out to sea.

PHONICS Alive at Home
Read the poem with your child. Ask your child to retell the story.

Name ________________________________

Six has the short **i** sound. Listen for the sound of short **i** in the rhyme.

Six fish swim.
Which one will win?
Will it be the fish
With the big pink fin?

Helpful Hint

If a syllable or word has only one vowel and it comes at the beginning or between two consonants, the vowel usually has the **short** sound.

Find and write the short **i** word that names each picture.

bib	fin	kiss	lid	list	milk
mitt	pin	rip	six	swim	wig

1	2	3	4
______	______	______	______
5	6	7	8 eggs bread milk juice apples
______	______	______	______
9	10	11	12
______	______	______	______

Say the name of each picture. Then read the words. Look at the phonogram in the words and write two more words with that phonogram.

1	2	3
pig big	kit hit	fin bin
4	**5**	**6**
lid bid	hill fill	kick lick

Work with a partner. Write a list of words that rhyme with **k**ing.

Write **_ig, _in,** and **_id** on a piece of paper. Ask your child to write words from this page under the correct heading.

Name ______________________________

Fill in the circle before the sentence that tells about the picture. Compare answers with a partner.

1	◯ Kit will learn to swim. ◯ Kit will learn to wink.
2	◯ She sips her milk fast. ◯ She kicks her feet fast.
3	◯ Will Kit sit well? ◯ Will Kit swim well?
4	◯ Ms. Hill gives Kit a tip. ◯ Ms. Hill gives Kit a wig.
5	◯ Now Kit can sniff like a fish. ◯ Now Kit can swish like a fish.
6	◯ Kit sits down to rest. ◯ Kit rests on a hill.
7	◯ Ms. Hill has a list for Kit. ◯ Ms. Hill has a gift for Kit.

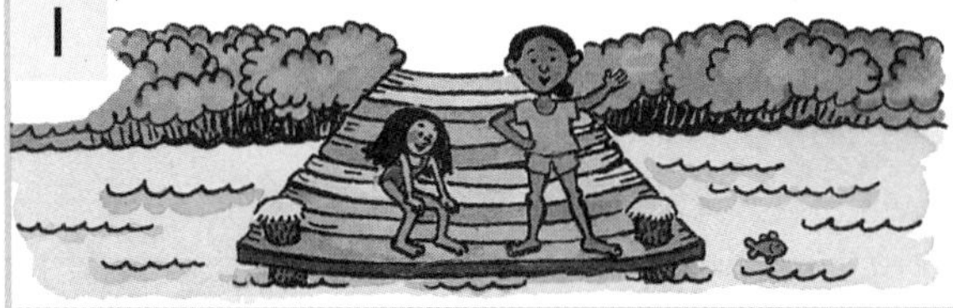

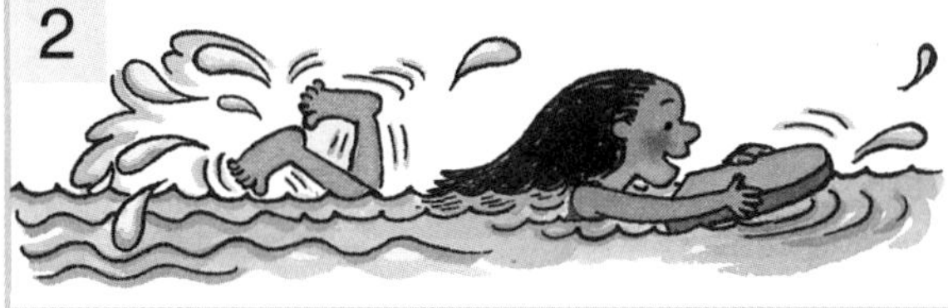

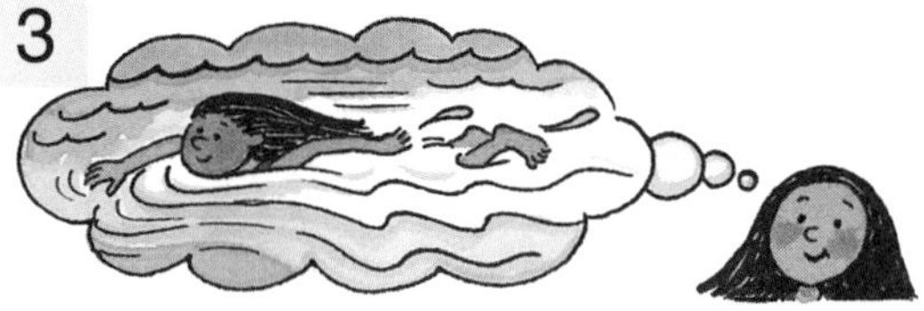

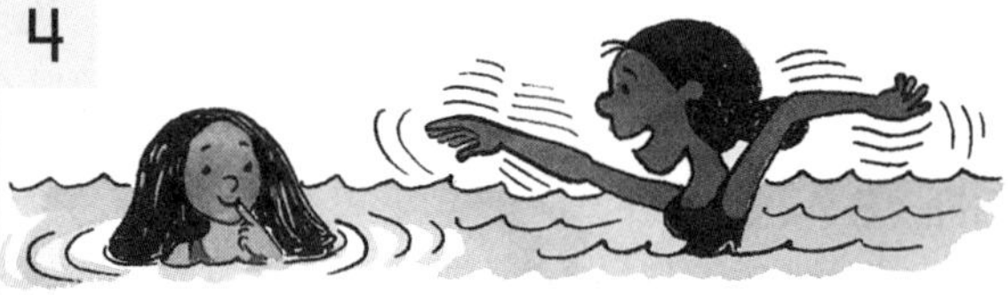

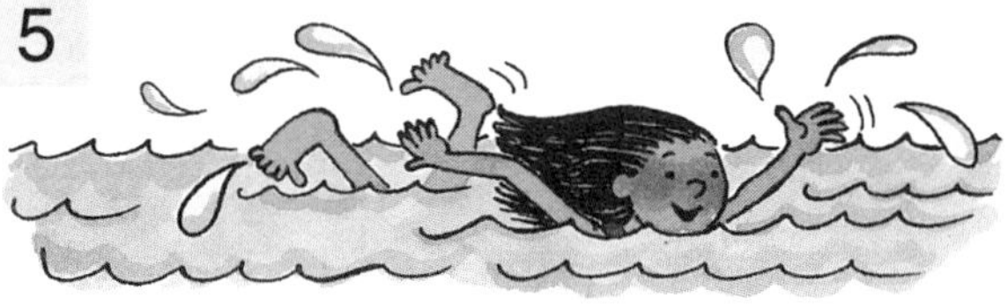

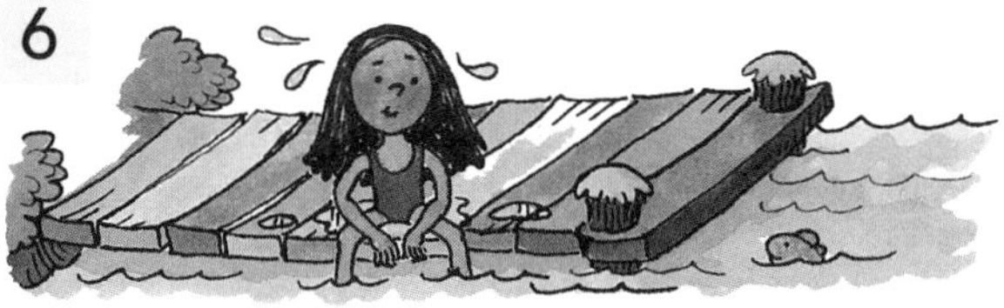

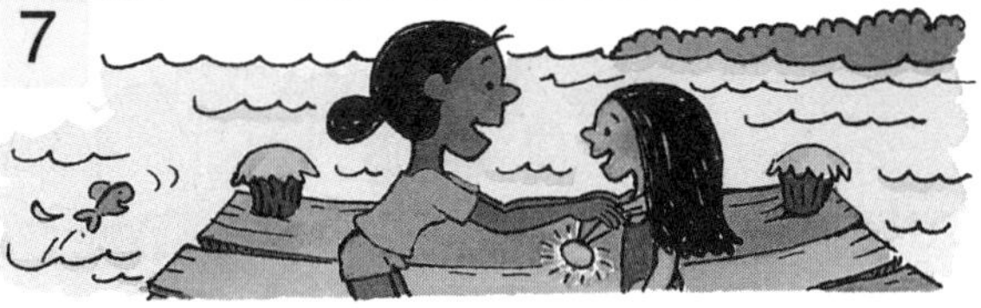

Draw a picture about swimming. Write one sentence that goes with the picture and one that does not. Ask someone to choose the correct sentence.

Read the poem. Underline the short **i** words. Then use short **i** words to complete the sentences.

Swish, Swish, Swish

Bill and Jill do not miss
A chance to see the giant fish.
Up and down the big fish swim.
Watch their fins go swish, swish, swish.

What a thrill for Jill and Bill
To see the fish go by.
In and out the big fish swim.
Watch their fins go swish, swish, swish.

1. Bill and Jill see giant ____________.

2. The fish ____________ up and down.

3. The fish swim ____________ and out.

4. The ____________ of the fish go swish, swish, swish.

PHONICS Alive at Home

Make up sentences with your child using short **i** words from the poem.

Name ______________________________

Dog has the short **o** sound. Listen for the sound of short **o** in the rhyme.

My dog Spot
Jumps in with a PLOP!
The frogs on the log
Jump and flip-flop.

Helpful Hint

If a syllable or word has only one vowel and it comes at the beginning or between two consonants, the vowel usually has the **short** sound.

Circle and write the short **o** word that names each picture. In the last box, draw a picture for a short **o** word. Write the word.

1 dot dog log	2 tot mop top	3 nod cob job
4 box fox hop	5 frog fog rot	6 rob cod rod
7 pot pop stop	8 jog cot not	9

Say the phonogram. Circle two pictures that have that phonogram in their names. Write the picture names.

1 _op	2 _og	3 _ot	4 _ock

Write a silly sentence with two rhyming short **o** words. Tell what you can see at a pond. For example, "I can see a wet **clock** on a **rock.**"

With your child, write a list of words that end in **ob.**

Name ______________________________

Work with a partner. Complete each sentence by writing the last three words in order.

1 to like golf

Mom and Pam ______________________.

2 a pond into

Mom hit the ball ______________________.

3 frog on a

They saw it land ______________________.

4 off rock the

"Mom, don't slip ______________________."

5 stop not did

But Mom ______________________.

6 a with plop

She fell in ______________________!

Read the poem. Underline the short **o** words. Then number the sentences to show the order of the things that happened.

At the Pond

Tom went to the pond
And sat on some rocks.
He put bait on his rod,
Then took off his socks.

Tom saw a frog on a log.
He said, "Please don't hop.
You'll scare the fish
If you don't stop."

_____ Tom saw a frog on a log.

_____ Tom went to the pond.

_____ Tom asked a frog not to hop.

_____ Tom took off his socks.

PHONICS Alive at Home

Talk about the poem with your child. Ask: What happened first? What happened next? What happened then?

Name ______________________________

Bug has the short **u** sound. Listen for the sound of short **u** in the rhyme.

A bug on a cup
Sailed in the sun.
A pup in a tub said,
"This is such fun!"

Helpful Hint

If a syllable or word has only one vowel and it comes at the beginning or between two consonants, the vowel usually has the **short** sound.

Find and write the short **u** word that names each picture.

bud	bun	bus	cup	gum	hump
hut	nut	plug	rug	run	tub

1 ______	2 ______	3 ______	4 ______
5 ______	6 ______	7 ______	8 ______
9 ______	10 ______	11 ______	12 ______

Say the name of each picture. Then read the words. Look at the phonogram in the words and write two more words with that phonogram.

1	2	3
bug mug	cut hut	sun fun

4	5	6
cub rub	drum sum	trunk bunk

Make up rhyming riddles for the words on this page. For example, "What rhymes with **fun** and shines in the sky?" (**sun**)

Ask your child to read the words he or she wrote. Together, think of other rhyming short **u** words.

Name ______________________________

Use a word from the box to complete each sentence.
Then take turns reading the sentences with a partner.

bumps	gulls	hums	run	stuff

Lucky Gus

1. Gus likes to ______________ on the beach.

2. He ______________ a song as he jogs.

3. He waves at the ______________ in the sky.

4. He looks for ______________ in the sand.

5. One day Gus ______________ into a trunk.

Lucky Gus! What do you think he finds in the trunk? Write about it.

____

____

____

Read the poem. Underline the short **u** words. Then use short **u** words to complete the sentences. Read each sentence and have a partner say the missing word.

Here Comes The Tug

I have a friend named Rusty.
He has a boat named Dusty.
Up and down the river she runs,
Giving free rides, just for fun.

Oh no, Rusty. What's that thud?
It's poor Dusty, stuck in mud.
Rusty, get the boat to run,
Or we'll sit here in the sun.

Don't fuss, Rusty. We're in luck.
Dusty soon will be unstuck.
Listen and you'll hear a chug.
Aren't you glad to see the tug?

1. Rusty's boat is named ______________.

2. Dusty got ______________ in the mud.

3. Dusty could not ______________.

4. A ______________ came to help.

Read the poem with your child. Ask: What was the problem? What was the solution?

Name ______________________________

Bell has the short **e** sound. Listen for the sound of short **e** in the rhyme.

This is Bess Bell,
The best swimmer yet.
Too bad Bess Bell
Hates to get wet.

Helpful Hint

If a syllable or word has only one vowel and it comes at the beginning or between two consonants, the vowel usually has the **short** sound.

Find and write the short **e** word that names each picture.

bell	desk	egg	hen	jet	leg
pet	sled	ten	vest	web	wet

1	2	3	4
5	6	7	8
9	10	11	12

Say the name of each picture. Then read the word. Look at the phonogram in the word and write another word with that phonogram.

1	2	3	4
bed	**m**en	**n**et	**b**eg
5	**6**	**7**	**8**
well	**n**est	**b**elt	**t**ent

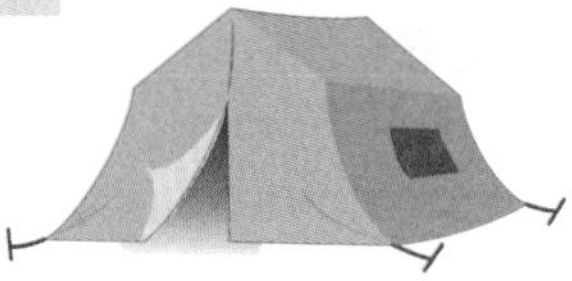

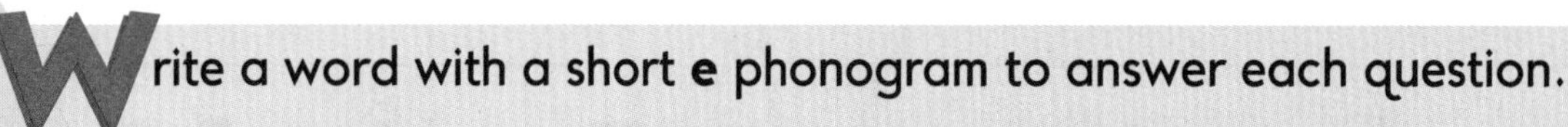

Write a word with a short **e** phonogram to answer each question.

9. What names a color and rhymes with **bed**? ______

10. What names a number and rhymes with **men**? ______

11. What gives you water and rhymes with **bell**? ______

12. What holds your pants up and rhymes with **melt**? ______

With your child, take turns asking and answering the questions at the bottom of the page.

Name ______________________________

Fill in the circle before the sentence that tells about the picture. Take turns reading your answers with a partner.

1 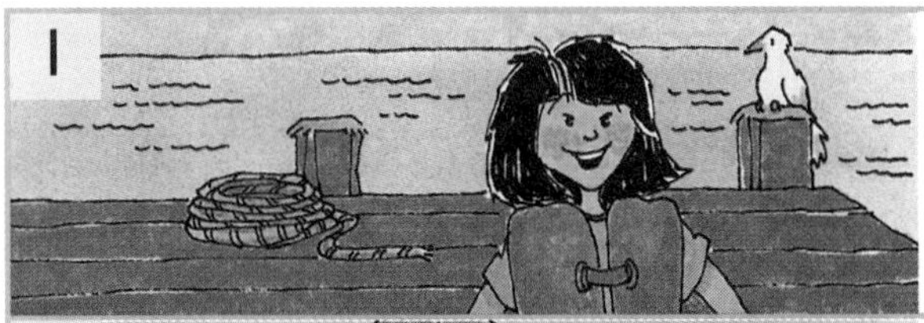
- ◯ Ming wears a dress.
- ◯ Ming wears a vest.

2 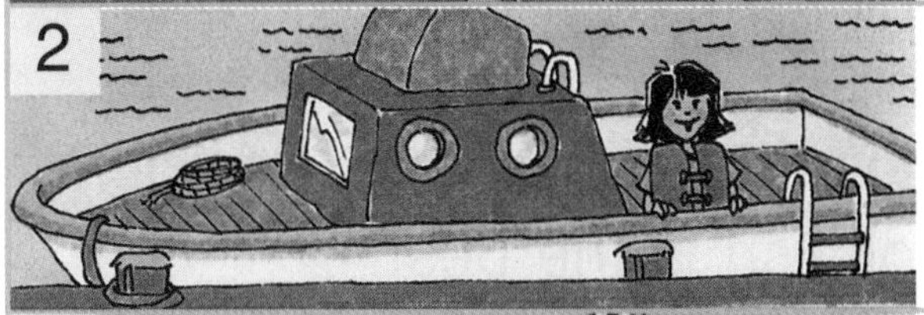
- ◯ She goes on deck.
- ◯ She goes to bed.

3 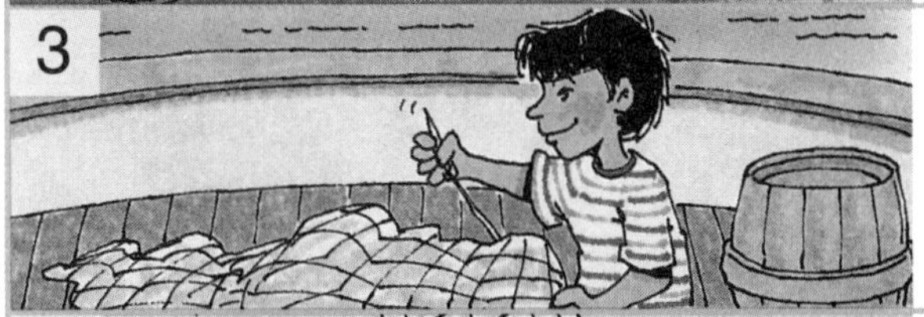
- ◯ Chen helps fix the desk.
- ◯ Chen helps mend the net.

4 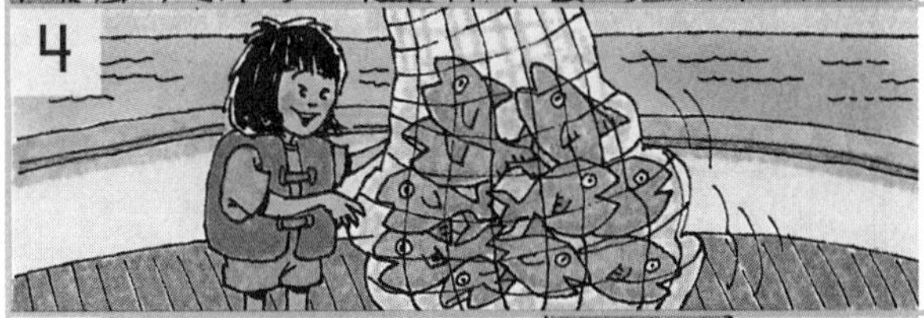
- ◯ Ming gets ten fish.
- ◯ Ming gets six eggs.

5 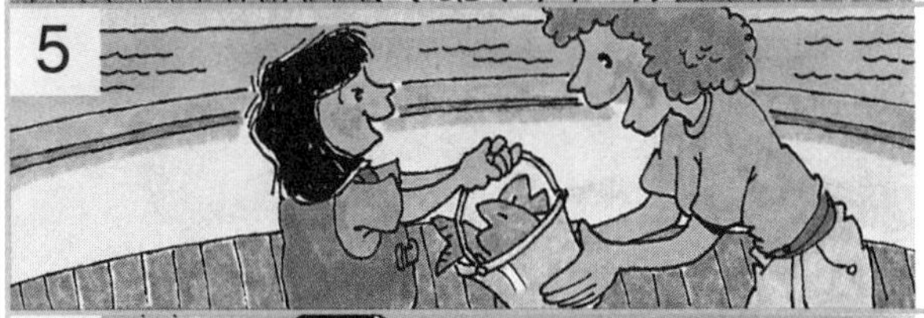
- ◯ They sell the last nest to Jen.
- ◯ They sell the best fish to Jen.

6 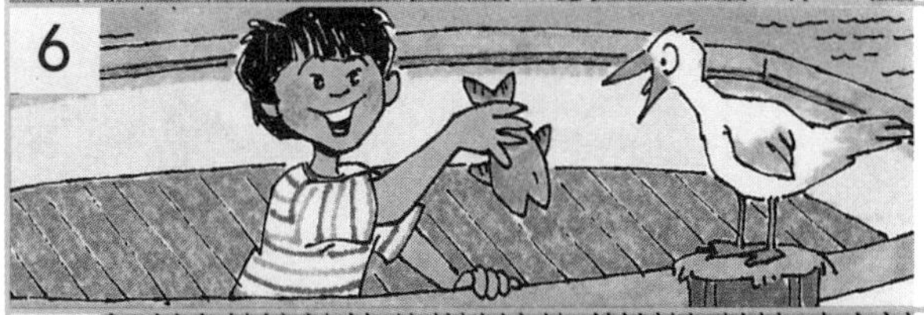
- ◯ The rest are fed to the gulls.
- ◯ The rest are led to the tent.

7 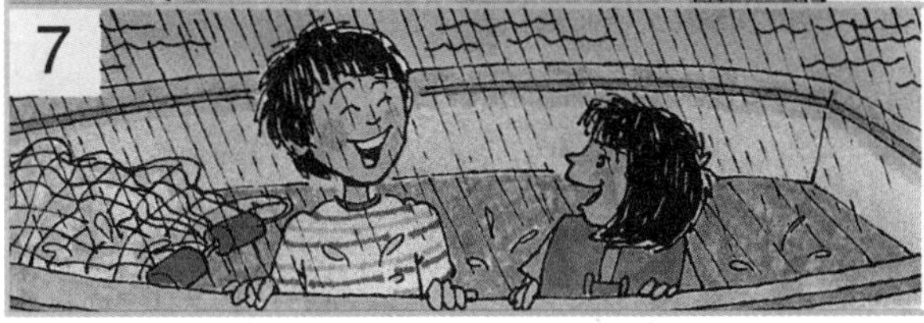
- ◯ Ming and Chen get wet.
- ◯ Ming and Chen go to the vet.

Draw a picture of Ming and Chen. Write one sentence that goes with the picture and one that does not. Ask someone to choose the correct sentence.

Read the poem. Underline the short **e** words. Then use short **e** words to complete the sentences.

The Best Pet

A goldfish doesn't need new toys
Or a ball of yarn that's red.
A goldfish doesn't need a dish
When it's being fed.
A goldfish doesn't need a bed
When it's time to rest.
I think, of all the pets around,
A goldfish is the best!

1. A goldfish doesn't need yarn that's __________.

2. A goldfish is not __________ from a dish.

3. A goldfish doesn't __________ in a bed.

4. A goldfish is the best __________.

LESSON 17: Short Vowel **e** in Context
Comprehension: Distinguishing Fact/Opinion

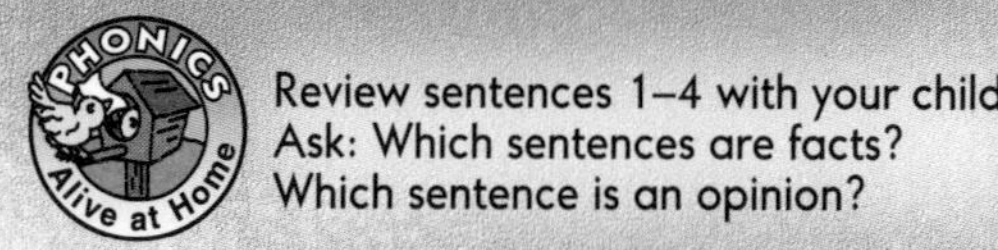

Review sentences 1–4 with your child. Ask: Which sentences are facts? Which sentence is an opinion?

Name ______________________________

Draw a line through three boxes in a row with words or pictures that have the same vowel sound. You can go across, down, or corner-to-corner.

1

map		
	job	pop
ham	lip	zip

2

trip		win
log		sag
	pot	hit

3

	log	crab
	hot	
bit	kiss	sag

4

	bill	
mitt	band	fad
mop	rob	

Write a short story. Pretend you're at a fishing pond with a friend. What happens there? Use some of these words in your story: **pal, sand, map, swim, wind, fish, rock, fog, dock.**

Unscramble the words to make sentences. Write each sentence.

1 into a puddle. Nell fell

2 very Nell wet. got

3 in water. Ducks day spend all

4 They ponds. jump into and puddles

5 bugs hunt for They in water.

6 lucky. are ducks But

7 do not Ducks wet! get

PHONICS Alive at Home

Ask your child to read his or her sentences to you.

Name ___________________________

Use a word from the box to complete each sentence. Then practice reading the sentences aloud.

around	because	does	right	wash	Why

1. ____________ is Pup a mess?

2. It is ____________ he ran in the mud.

3. I can ____________ Pup in a big tub.

4. But Pup ____________ not like to get wet.

5. So I will put mud ____________ the tub.

6. Pup will jump ____________ in!

Use one or more words from the box to answer the questions.

7. Why is Pup a mess?

____

8. Why will Pup jump in the tub?

____

Read the story. Then answer the questions.

Why Sun and Moon Are in the Sky

Long ago, Sun and Moon lived in a small hut on Earth. Water lived far away.

One day Sun went to see Water. "Come visit us," said Sun. "We will make our hut big so you can fit in it."

When the hut was ready, Water came to visit. Moon was afraid. "We will get wet," Moon said.

Moon was right. Water filled up the hut. Everything got wet.

Sun and Moon ran to the top of the roof. Moon grabbed Sun's hand. They jumped into the sky, where they are still safe and happy today.

1. Where did Sun and Moon live on Earth?

2. Why was Moon afraid of Water's visit?

LESSON 20: Connecting Reading and Writing
Comprehension: Identifying the Setting

PHONICS Alive at Home

Read the story with your child. Ask: Where did Sun and Moon live at the end of the story? Why did they leave Earth?

Name ______________________________

Spell, Write, and Tell

Say, spell, and talk about each word in the box. Then write each word under the short vowel sound in its name.

big
cut
did
fox
got
has
let
ran
ten
tug

1 Short **a**

2 Short **i**

3 Short **o**

4 Short **u**

5 Short **e**

The pictures tell a story. Draw a picture to show what happens next. Then write a sentence to go with each picture. Use one or more of your spelling words. Share your sentences with the class.

big	cut	did	fox	got	has	let	ran	ten	tug

1

2

3

Make up sentences with your child using the spelling words on this page.

Name ___________________________

Let's read and talk about Niagara Falls.

Welcome to Niagara Falls. These falls are in New York and in Canada. Do you want to see the top? Visit the tower on the New York side. Watch the water rush right down with a crash.

Would you like a closer look? Put on a raincoat and ride around on the boat called *Maid of the Mist*. But don't get upset if you get wet!

What else would you like to know about Niagara Falls?

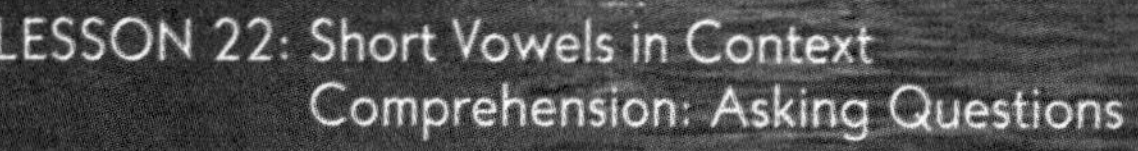

Check-Up

Fill in the circle next to the word that names the picture.

1. ○ fun ○ fan ○ fin
2. ○ big ○ bag ○ bug
3. ○ pig ○ pug ○ peg
4. ○ leg ○ lag ○ log
5. ○ bud ○ bed ○ bid
6. ○ not ○ nut ○ net
7. ○ list ○ lost ○ last
8. ○ hum ○ him ○ ham
9. ○ wall ○ will ○ well
10. ○ cab ○ cub ○ cob
11. ○ led ○ lad ○ lid
12. ○ sock ○ sick ○ sack
13. ○ tan ○ tin ○ ten
14. ○ tap ○ top ○ tip
15. ○ hit ○ hut ○ hat

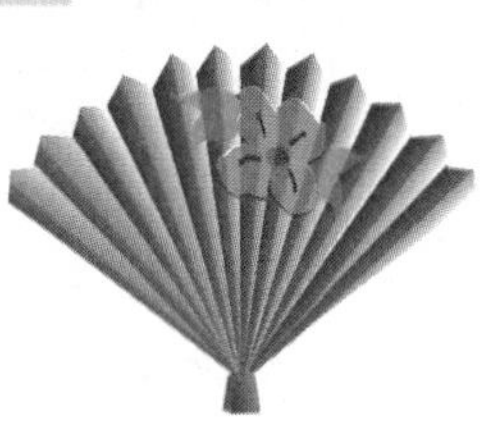

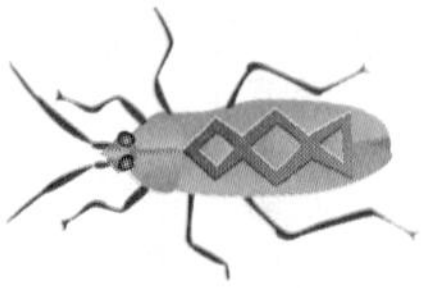

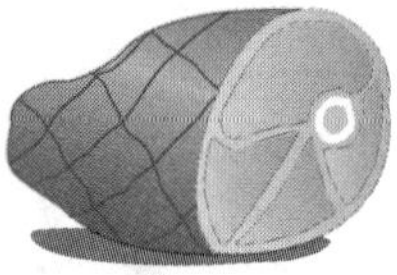

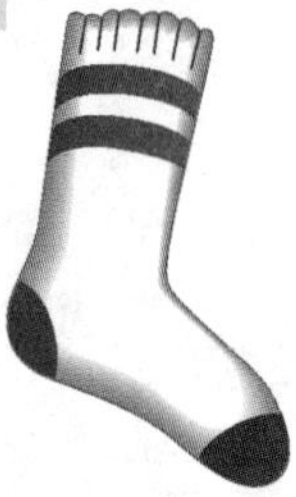

PHONICS Alive at Home

Review this Check-Up with your child.

TREES

Trees are the kindest things I know,
They do no harm, they simply grow

And spread a shade for sleepy cows,
And gather birds among their boughs.

They give us fruit in leaves above,
And wood to make our houses of,

And leaves to burn on Hallowe'en,
And in the Spring new buds of green.

They are the first when day's begun
To touch the beams of morning sun,

They are the last to hold the light
When evening changes into night,

And when a moon floats on the sky
They hum a drowsy lullaby

Of sleepy children long ago...
Trees are the kindest things I know.

Harry Behn

Critical Thinking

In what other ways are trees kind?
What can you do to be kind to trees?

Name ______________________________________

Visit us at
www.sadlier-oxford.com

Dear Family,

As your child progresses through this unit about trees and nature, he or she will review the long vowel sounds of **a**, **i**, **o**, **u**, and **e**.

• Say the picture names together and listen to the long vowel sounds. Long vowels say their own names.

Apreciada Familia:

En esta unidad, acerca de la naturaleza, su niño repasará los sonidos largos de las vocales **a**, **i**, **o**, **u**, **e**.

• Pronuncien el nombre de las cosas y escuchen el sonido largo de las vocales. El sonido largo es como el nombre de la vocal.

a	i	o	u	e
				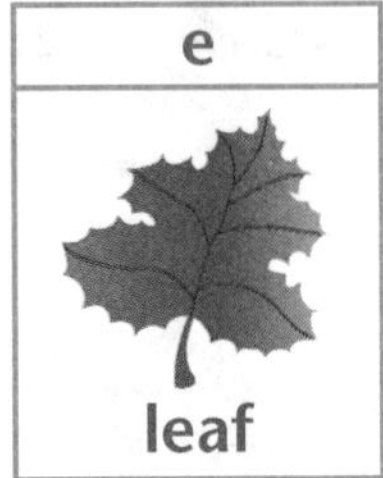
rain	vine	rose	fruit	leaf

• Read the poem "Trees" on the reverse side. Talk about ways that trees help us.

• Ask your child to find the rhyming words at the end of each pair of lines, for example: know and grow.

• Help your child find some of the long vowel words in the poem. (trees, know, grow, shade, sleepy, fruit, leaves, make, green, beams, floats)

• Lea la poesía "Trees" en la página 47. Hablen sobre cómo los árboles nos ayudan.

• Pida al niño encontrar la palabra que rima al final de cada par de versos, por ejemplo: know y grow.

• Ayude al niño a encontrar algunas palabras donde el sonido de la vocal es largo. (trees, know, grow, shade, sleepy, fruit, leaves, make, green, beams, floats)

PROJECT

Make a word tree from a small branch that has fallen off a tree. Place the branch in a can filled with dirt or clay. Then have your child draw leaves and cut them out. He or she can write new long vowel words on the leaves and attach them to the tree.

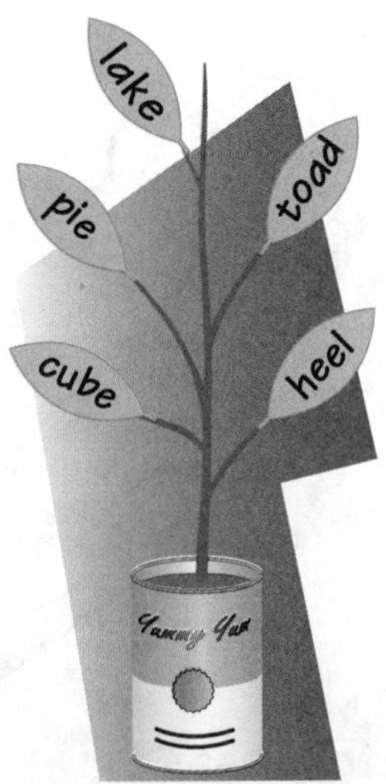

PROYECTO

Haga un árbol de palabras. Consiga una ramita y póngala en una lata llena de tierra o barro. Haga que el niño dibuje hojas y las recorte. A medida que el niño vaya aprendiendo palabras donde el sonido de las vocales es largo, puede escribirlas en las hojas y atarlas al árbol con un cordón.

Name ____

Race has the long **a** sound. Listen for the sound of long **a** in the rhyme.

Two snakes had a race one day,
Way to the top of a vine.
"Wait! Wait!" I heard one say.
"Is that your tail or mine?"

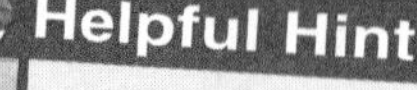

If there are two vowels in a one-syllable word, the first vowel is usually **long** and the second vowel is silent. There are different ways to spell long **a**.

The letters **a_e** can stand for the long **a** sound. If the name of the picture has the long **a** sound, write **a** in the middle and **e** at the end of the word.

1 t p	2 l k	3 h t
4 j m	5 c n	6 g m
7 c v	8 m p	9 r k

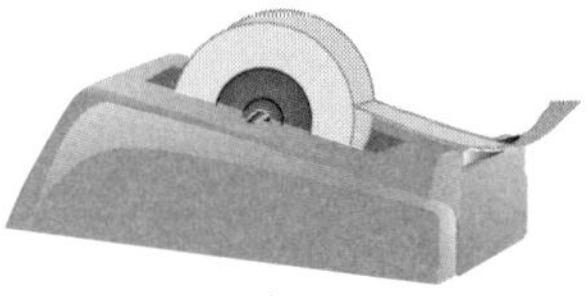

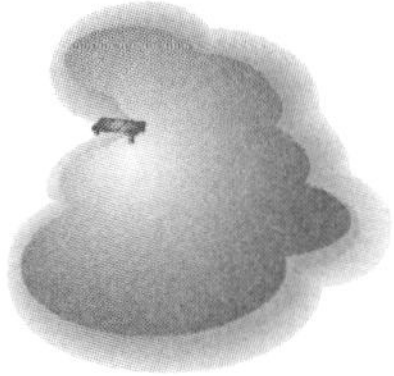

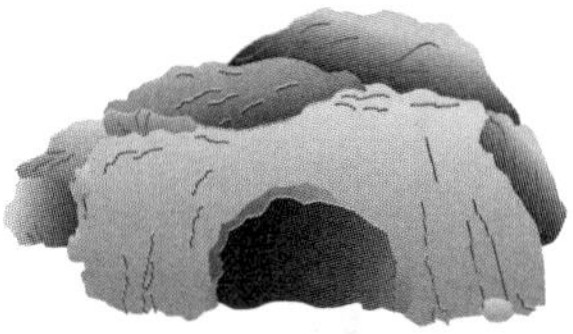

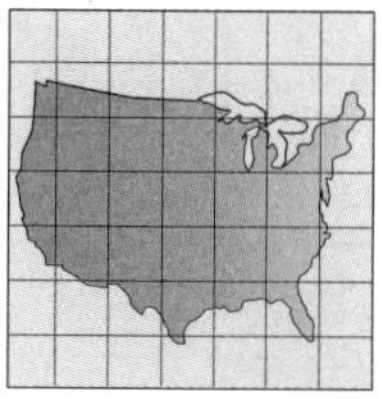

The letters **ai** and **ay** can stand for the long **a** sound. If the name of the picture has the long **a** sound, write **ai** or **ay** to complete the word.

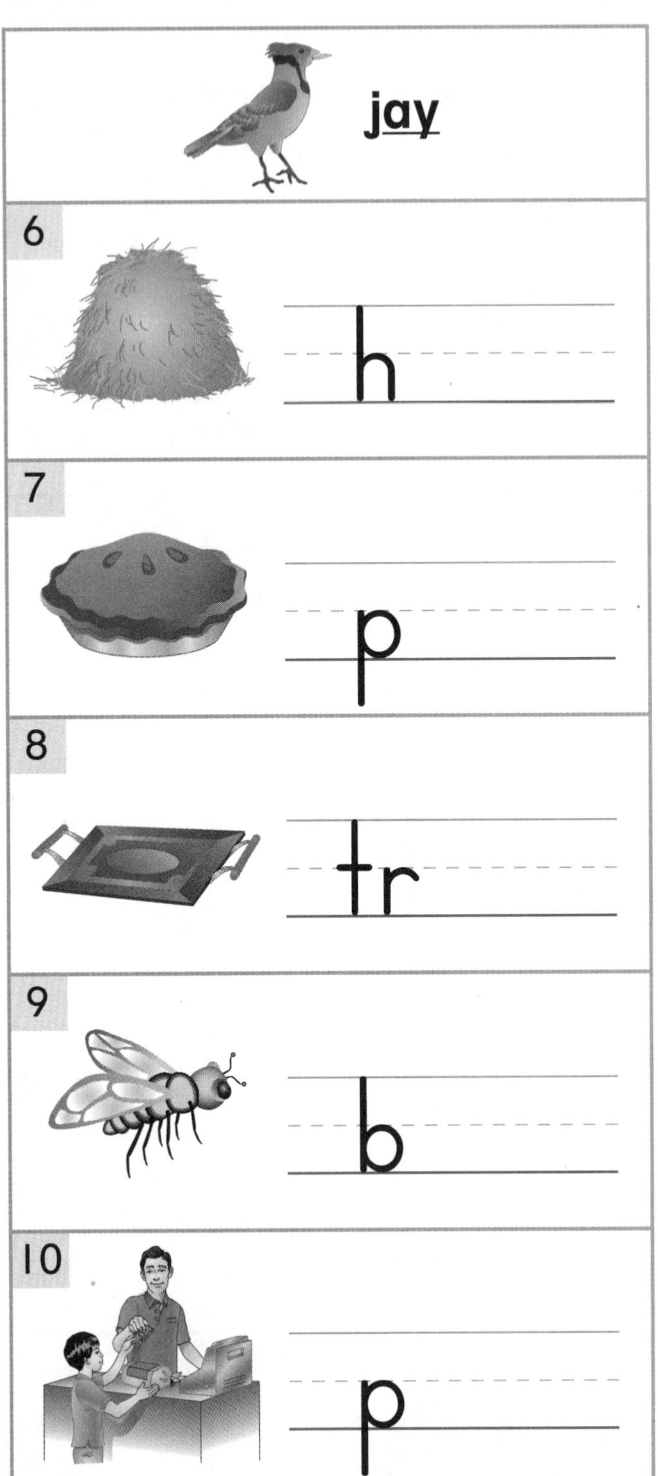

pail

jay

1 t l

2 r n

3 j p

4 n l

5 tr n

6 h

7 p

8 tr

9 b

10 p

What would you p**ai**nt on a r**ai**ny d**ay**? Write about it. Begin your sentence, "On a rainy day I would paint . . . ."

PHONICS Alive at Home

Ask your child to read the words he or she wrote.

Name ____________________

Color the raindrops that have long **a** words.

Circle and write the long **a** word that names each picture.

1	2	3
cake cane can	ran rain rate	hay ham hat
4	**5**	**6**
pal pail pan	game gap gate	jail jam jay
7	**8**	**9**
cap came cape	pad pay pal	sat same sail

Say each phonogram. Then say the name of the picture and write the word. Add another word with the same phonogram.

1 _ake	2 _ail	3 _ay
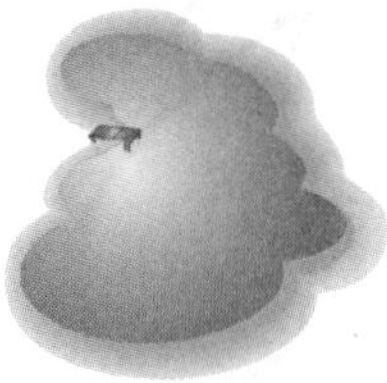		

Say the phonogram at the beginning of each row. Circle the words with that phonogram. Then write another word with the same phonogram.

4. _ave save sat wave
5. _ain pan pain main
6. _ate late date bat
7. _ame jam same tame

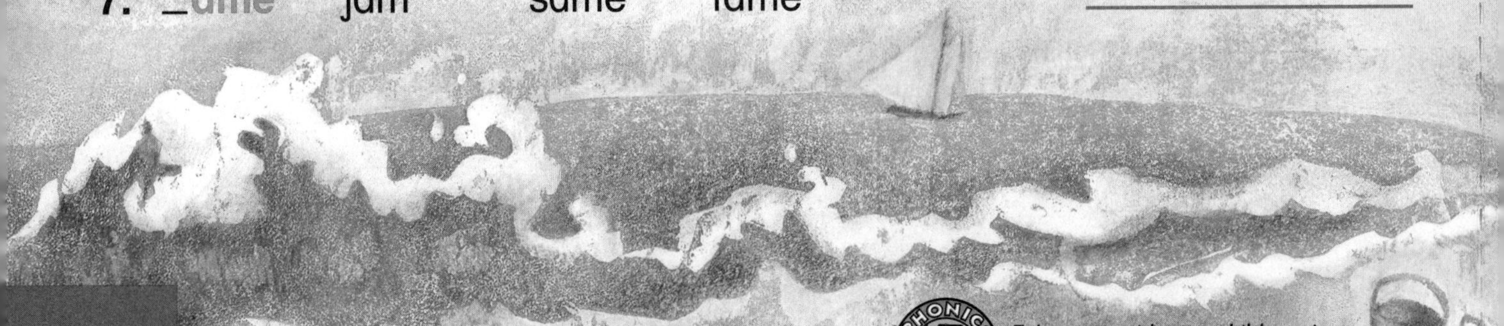

Take turns with your child naming words that rhyme with **day.**

Name ________________________________

Look at the picture. Circle and write the word that completes the sentence. Have a partner name the letters that stand for the long **a** sound in each circled word.

1	We go to the ____________.	make lake lay
2	We ____________ in a boat.	sail save pail
3	We play a ____________.	game gave wave
4	We ____________ lunch.	make bake mail
5	Then the ____________ comes down.	ray rail rain
6	But we ____________ dry.	way stay wait

Read the poem. Underline the long **a** words. Then use long **a** words to complete the sentences.

Grandpa Jake's Farm

I'm swinging from a tree.
I'm jumping in the hay.
I'm feeding chicks and pigs today,
And watching goats at play.

I'm here at Grandpa Jake's farm,
I really cannot wait
To race down to the lake and take
My pail and lots of bait.

1. The girl is jumping in the ______________.

2. She cannot ______________ to go fishing.

3. She will fish in a ______________.

4. She needs lots of ______________ to fish.

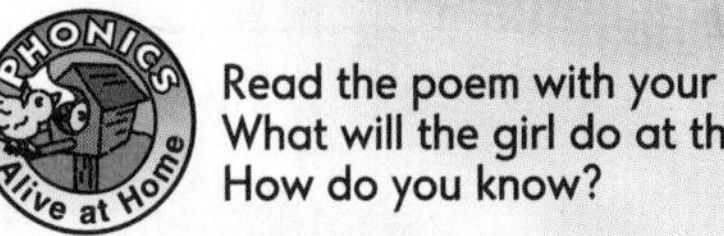

Read the poem with your child. Ask: What will the girl do at the lake? How do you know?

Name ______________________________

Pine has the long **i** sound. Listen for the sound of long **i** in the rhyme.

The fine pine rises high,
Up to skies so blue.
If it gets just twice as tall,
It will slice right through!

Helpful Hint

If there are two vowels in a one-syllable word, the first vowel is usually **long** and the second vowel is silent. There are different ways to spell long **i**.

The letters **i_e, ie,** and **igh** can stand for the long **i** sound. Circle the words in the box that have the long **i** sound. Then sort the long **i** words according to their spelling pattern.

bite	high	hill	lid	
lie	mile	night	rip	
ripe	sigh	tie	wig	

kite	pie	light
______	______	______
______	______	______
______	______	______

Say the phonogram. Circle the pictures that have that phonogram in their names. Then write the words.

1 _ine	2 _ie	3 _ime	4 _ide

Change these short **i** words into long **i** words by adding a final **e: kit, pin, fin, rid, hid, bit.** Write the words under the correct heading: **_ite, _ine,** or **_ide.**

With your child, take turns writing long **i** words by changing the first letter in **bike** and **hive.**

Name ______________________

Work with a partner to complete each sentence by choosing two long **i** words that make sense. One partner can write the first word, and the other partner can write the second word.

1 tie Pine like

We ________ Camp ________ Tree.

2 ride pile bikes

We ________ our ________ up a hill.

3 five pie hike

We ________ for ________ miles.

4 high kite dive

We fly a ________ way up ________.

5 hive lie bright

We ________ under ________ stars.

6 vine night time

It's ________ to say good ________.

Read the poem. Underline the long **i** words. Then number the sentences in order to tell what to do.

Time to Dine

Make a fine bird feeder,
Tie it tightly with twine,
And hang it way up high
From a wide, tall tree.

Now hide and stay quite still.
For in a little while,
The birds will come to dine.
Just wait and you will see!

___ Hang the feeder up high.

___ Make a fine bird feeder.

___ Hide so the birds don't see you.

___ Tie twine to the bird feeder.

LESSON 28: Long Vowel **i** in Context
Comprehension: Identifying Steps in a Process

PHONICS Alive at Home

Talk about the poem. Ask your child to tell what to do first, second, third, and last if you want to see lots of birds.

Name ____________________

Home has the long **o** sound. Listen for the sound of long **o** in the rhyme.

A crow sat at home,
Alone in an oak,
A fine dark shadow
In a black cloak.

Helpful Hint

If there are two vowels in a one-syllable word, the first vowel is usually **long** and the second vowel is silent. There are different ways to spell long **o**.

The letters **o_e** can stand for the long **o** sound. If the name of the picture has the long **o** sound, write **o** in the middle and **e** at the end of the word.

1 b n	2 r b	3 d g
4 h s	5 g t	6 r p
7 f x	8 c n	9 sm k

The letters **oa, ow,** and **oe** can stand for the long **o** sound. Sort the long **o** words according to their spelling patterns.

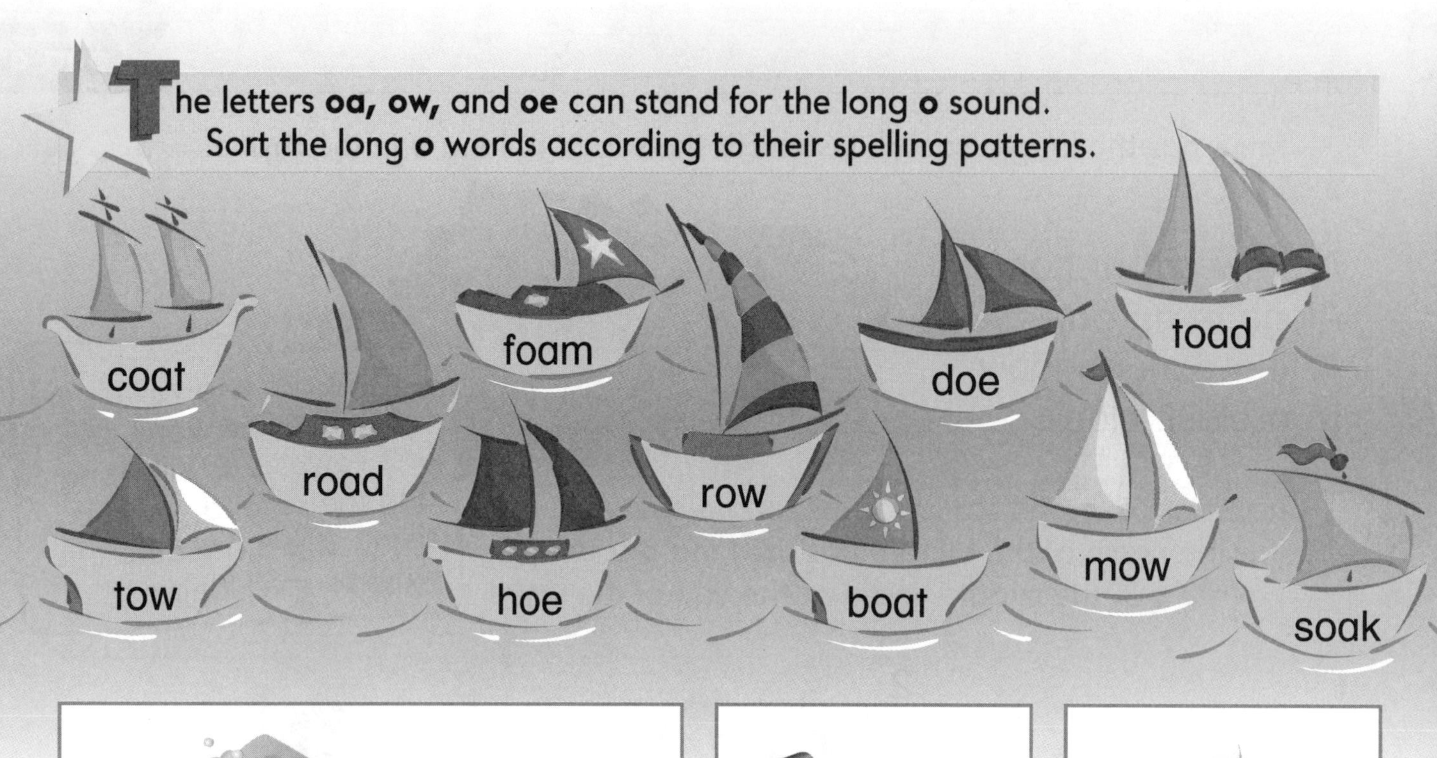

 soap		 bow	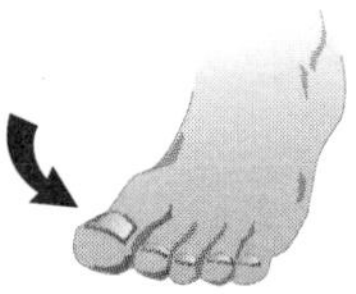 toe
1	4	7	10
2	5	8	11
3	6	9	

Write about a **boa**t trip that you would like to take.

LESSON 29: Connecting Sound to Symbol: /ō/ **oa, ow, oe**

Write the words **loan, lot,** and **low.** Ask your child to circle the two long **o** words. Repeat with **roam, row, rob.**

Name ______________________________

Color the roses that have long **o** words.

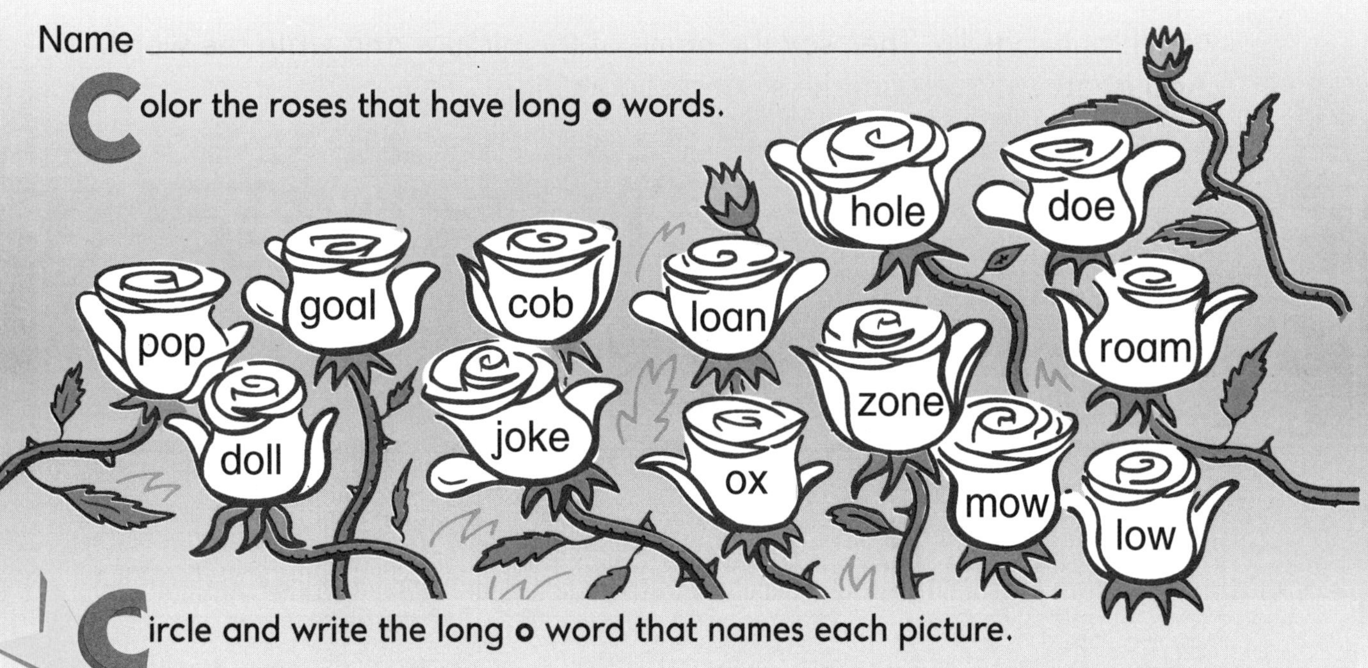

Circle and write the long **o** word that names each picture.

1 gap goat got	2 rose rob rod	3 boat box bow
4 hop hope hoe	5 robe row rope	6 note not nod
7 rod role road	8 toe top tone	9 bowl bin bone

Say each phonogram. Then say the name of the picture and write the word. Add another word with the same phonogram.

1 _oe	2 _oad	3 _one

Say the phonogram at the beginning of each row. Circle the words with that phonogram. Then write another word with the same phonogram.

4. _oat boat cot float
5. _ow rod tow snow
6. _oke poke woke wake
7. _ose hose hope nose

PHONICS Alive at Home

Have your child point to and read a long **o** word on the page and then say a rhyming word.

Name ____________________

Complete each sentence by writing the last three words in order. Then explain to a partner how the children planted a tree.

1

oak little tree

We have a ____________________.

2

a hoe with

I can dig ____________________.

3

make hole a

I will ____________________.

4

hose a use

Joan can ____________________.

5

tree the soak

She will ____________________.

6

grow will big

The oak ____________________.

Read the poem. Underline the long **o** words. Then use long **o** words to complete the sentences.

Hope for a Snow Day

It's starting to snow.
The wind will soon blow.
Joe thinks, "Will the school bus
Be able to go?"

Joe can't see the road.
The oak tree is white.
Joe hopes that the snow
Will fall through the night!

1. It's starting to ______________.

2. Joe can't see the ______________.

3. The ______________ tree is white.

4. Joe ______________ for a snow day.

LESSON 31: Long Vowel **o** in Context
Comprehension: Understanding Cause and Effect

Read the first verse of the poem and have your child read the second. Ask: What happens when it snows all night?

Name ____

Look at the picture. Then follow the directions below.

Directions

1. Color the lake blue.
2. Draw a road by the lake.
3. Circle the boat.
4. Color the pine tree green.
5. Draw a box around the kite.
6. Color each rose yellow.
7. Color the pail gray.
8. Draw a hole for the mole.
9. Draw a line over the stone.
10. Make an X on the hive.
11. Color the toad brown.
12. Draw a tail on the fox.

Check-Up

Color the box that contains the long vowel sound in each picture name. Write the word.

1
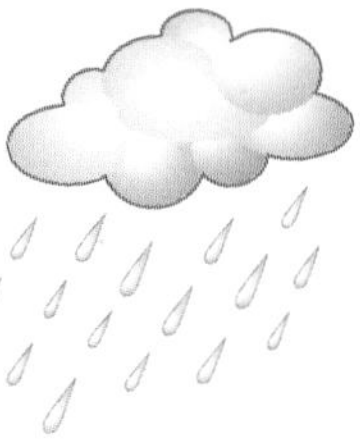
a
i
o

2
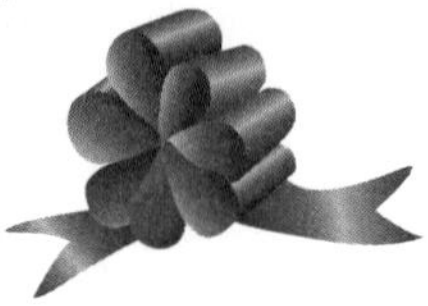
a
i
o

3
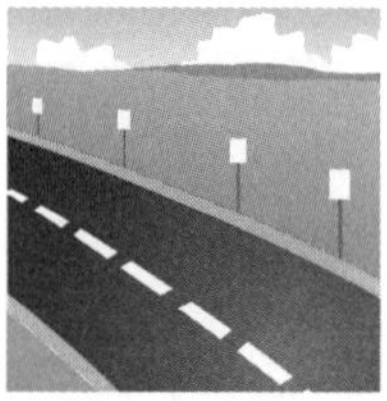
a
i
o

4
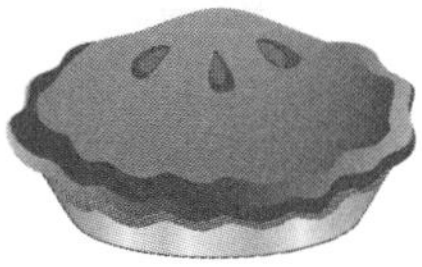
a
i
o

5
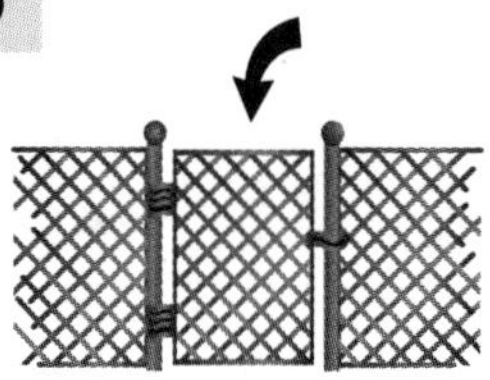
a
i
o

6
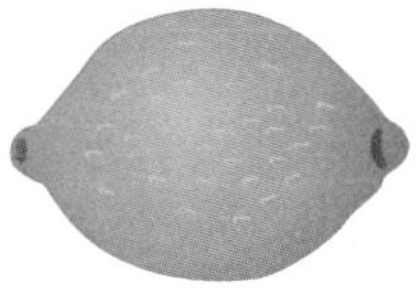
a
i
o

7
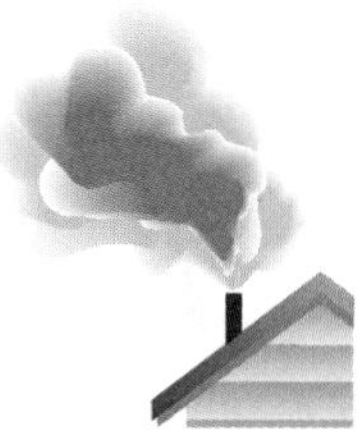
a
i
o

8
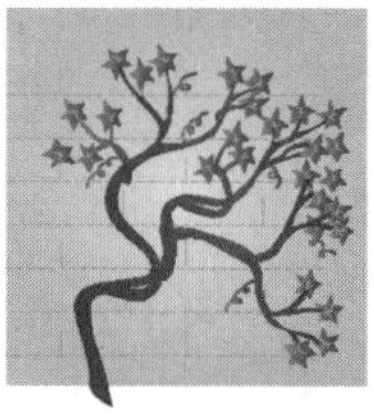
a
i
o

9
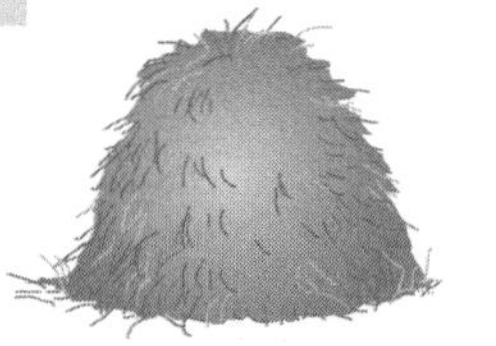
a
i
o

10
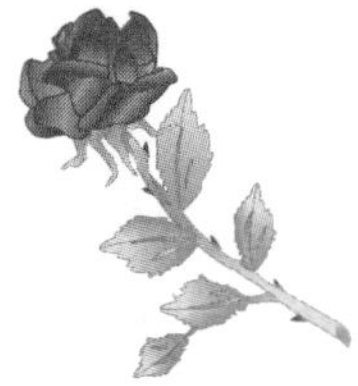
a
i
o

11
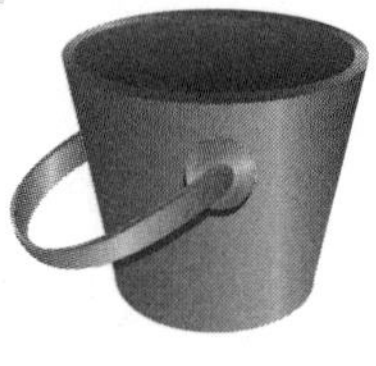
a
i
o

12
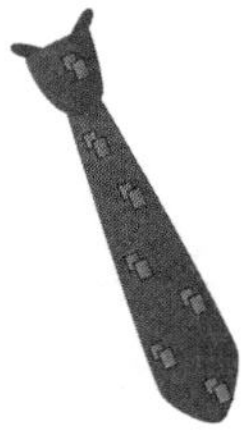
a
i
o

Review this Check-Up with your child.

Name ______________________________

June has the long **u** sound. Listen for the sound of long **u** in the rhyme.

Sue's fruit tree in June
Is so huge and so tall
That we can drink fruit juice
Spring, summer, and fall.

The letters **u_e, ui,** and **ue** can stand for the long **u** sound. Circle the words in the box that have the long **u** sound. Then sort the long **u** words according to their spelling pattern.

Helpful Hint

If there are two vowels in a one-syllable word, the first vowel is usually **long** and the second vowel is silent. There are different ways to spell long **u.**

blue	bun	buzz	clue	cut	cute
due	gum	juice	rule	suit	tune

 mule	 fruit	 glue
________	________	________
________	________	________
________	________	________
________		________

Say the phonogram. Circle the pictures that have that phonogram in their names. Then write the words.

1 _ube	2 _une	3 _uit	4 _ue

Work with a partner and write riddles for long **u** words. For example, "What comes from an orange?" (juice)

Ask your child to say the name of a picture he or she circled and then say a rhyming word.

Name ____________________

The underlined word in each sentence does not make sense. Find the word that does make sense on an orange and write it on the line. With a partner, take turns reading the sentences with the correct words.

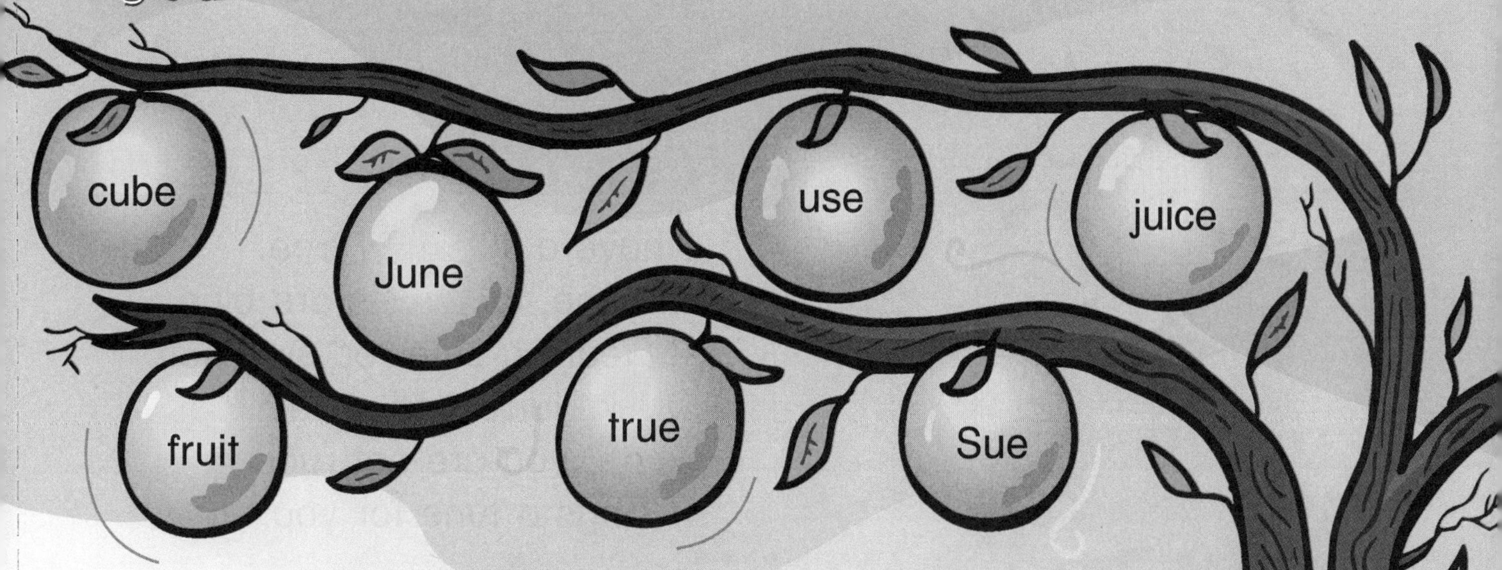

cube June use juice fruit true Sue

1. We have a big frog tree. ____________

2. The fruit will grow in Jim. ____________

3. In the fall, we can tune the fruit. ____________

4. We can make jam to drink. ____________

5. On hot days, we add an ice cub. ____________

6. Even baby suit drinks juice. ____________

7. We love our tree—it's blue! ____________

Read the poem. Underline the long **u** words. Then use long **u** words to complete the sentences.

Can This Be True?

I have a little fruit tree.
In June, its leaves are blue.
It wears a cute red swimsuit,
Drinks juice and water, too.
And if you are not rude to it,
It sings a tune for you.

1. The ____________ tree is little.

2. Its leaves are ____________.

3. Do not be ____________ to the tree.

4. It will sing a ____________ for you.

LESSON 34: Long Vowel **u** in Context
Comprehension: Distinguishing Fantasy/Reality

PHONICS Alive at Home

Read the poem with your child.
Ask: Is the fruit tree in the poem real or make-believe? How can you tell?

Name ______________________________

Leaves has the long **e** sound. Listen for the sound of long **e** in the rhyme.

I see beech leaves.
Let's put them in a heap.
Sweep them up neatly,
Then take a giant leap!

Helpful Hint

If there are two vowels in a one-syllable word, the first vowel is usually **long** and the second vowel is silent. There are different ways to spell long **e**.

The letters **ee** and **ea** can stand for the long **e** sound. If the name of the picture has the long **e** sound, write **ee** or **ea** to complete the word.

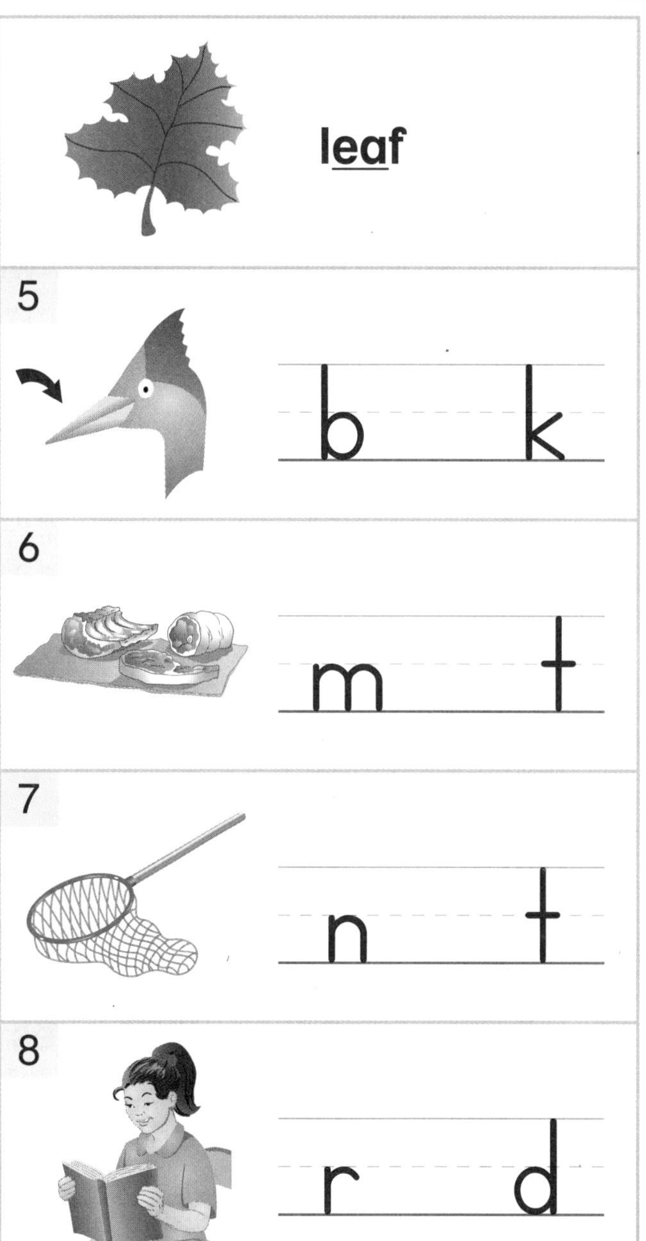

Say each phonogram. Then say the name of the picture and write the word.

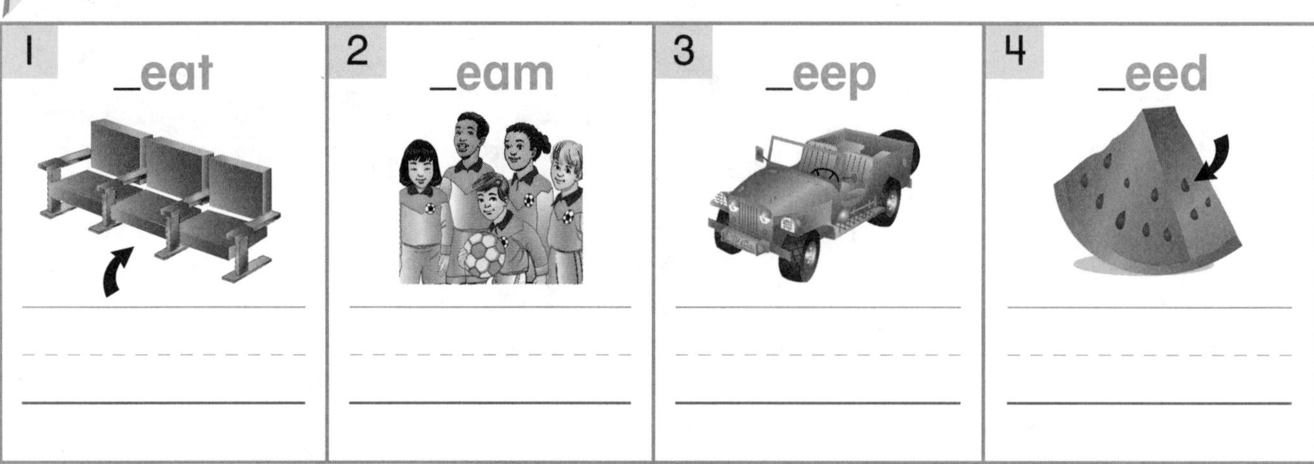

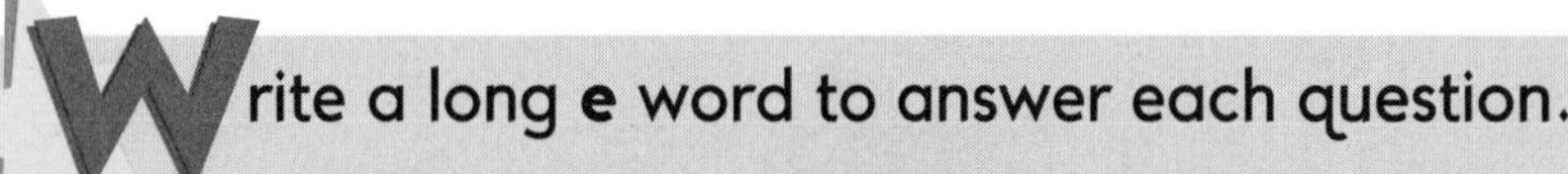

Write a long e word to answer each question.

5. What kind of insect rhymes with **see**? ________

6. What part of your foot rhymes with **feel**? ________

7. What part of a plant rhymes with **reed**? ________

8. What kind of animal rhymes with **real**? ________

9. What part of a bird rhymes with **leak**? ________

10. What part of a month rhymes with **peek**? ________

Write a silly question that begins "Have you ever seen . . .?" Use as many long **e** words as possible. For example, "Have you ever **seen** a **tree** of **green beans**?"

Take turns with your child asking and answering the questions on the page.

Name ______________________

Work Together

Fill in the circle next to the word that completes the sentence. Write the word in the sentence. Then read the sentences and have a partner name the long **e** words.

1. You can ____________ a lot in a tree.
   - ○ see
   - ○ seal

2. Let's take a ____________.
   - ○ neat
   - ○ peek

3. A mother bird has food in her ____________.
   - ○ bead
   - ○ beak

4. Baby birds ____________ in their nest.
   - ○ feet
   - ○ peep

5. Bugs run on each ____________.
   - ○ leaf
   - ○ feel

6. Squirrels ____________ nuts.
   - ○ meet
   - ○ eat

7. Squirrels ____________ and play all day.
   - ○ leap
   - ○ peel

Read the poem. Underline the long **e** words. Then use long **e** words to complete the sentences.

Please call the Clean Team.
Call us and you'll see,
We're the ones to make your yard
As neat as yards can be.

We'll rake up all the leaves that fall,
We'll work quite hard,
And—best of all—
We do it all for free.

1. Call the ______________ Team.

2. They will make your yard ______________.

3. The Clean Team will rake up ______________.

4. The Clean Team works for ______________.

Talk about the poem with your child. Ask: What is this poem all about?

Name ___

Remember

Combine words from boxes 1, 2, and 3 to write sentences. How many different sentences can you write?

1	2	3
Sweet Sue Queen Jean Mr. Green	plays the flute rides a mule plants a tree	on a dune. each June. on the street.

Color the box that contains the long vowel sound in each picture name. Write the word.

1	2	3
u / e	u / e	u / e
4	5	6
u / e	u / e	u / e
7	8	9
u / e	u / e	u / e
10	11	12
u / e	u / e	u / e

PHONICS Alive at Home Review this Check-Up with your child.

Name ____

Use a word from the box to complete each sentence.
Then practice reading the sentences aloud.

Don't	found	green	its	sing	use

1. A jay can sit in it and ______________.

2. A hive can be ______________ in it.

3. You can see a ______________ leaf on it.

4. You can ______________ it to make a bat.

5. You can use it for hide and seek. ______________ peek!

6. Can you say ______________ name?

Use one or more words from the box to answer the questions.

7. What can sing in a tree?

____

8. What have you found in a tree?

____

Read the story. Then answer the questions.

Johnny Appleseed

Johnny Appleseed lived a long time ago. Do you know the good things that he did?

Johnny wanted apple trees to grow all over America. So, as a young man, Johnny left his home. He walked across the land planting apple trees.

Johnny was nice to people. He gave them apple seeds and trees to plant. He did not make poor people pay for them. He wanted them to have fruit to eat.

Years later, Johnny returned to the places he had been. He was proud to see apple trees growing there. Apple trees may still be there today!

1. What was one way Johnny Appleseed was nice to people?

2. How can you be like Johnny Appleseed?

Together, talk about the things Johnny Appleseed did. Ask: Would you want him to be your friend? Why or why not?

Name ______________________________

Say, spell, and talk about each word in the box. Then write each word under the long vowel sound in its name.

coat
eat
five
fruit
home
make
may
pie
tree
tune

1 Long **a**	2 Long **i**	3 Long **o**
______	______	______
______	______	______

4 Long **u**
______
______

5 Long **e**
______
______

Make a list of things to do as you sit under an apple tree. Use two or more of your spelling words. Then share your favorite items with the class.

coat	eat	five	fruit	home
make	may	pie	tree	tune

Things To Do

hum a tune

LESSON 40: Connecting Spelling, Writing, and Speaking

Ask your child to read the items on the list and to point out the spelling words he or she used.

Name ______________________________

Let's read and talk about a tree named General Sherman.

Did you ever hug a tree? Could you reach all the way around its trunk? Not if you hugged General Sherman! General Sherman is the name of a giant sequoia tree. It is the biggest tree in California. In fact, it is the biggest tree in the world. General Sherman's trunk is very, very wide. It would take about 25 children holding hands to make a circle around this huge tree.

How would you feel standing next to General Sherman in a forest of giant green sequoia trees?

Check-Up Fill in the circle next to the word that names the picture.

1 ◯ van ◯ vane ◯ vine	2 ◯ glue ◯ clue ◯ glum	3 ◯ hat ◯ hay ◯ high
4 ◯ said ◯ seed ◯ see	5 ◯ rope ◯ slow ◯ row	6 ◯ tube ◯ tub ◯ tune
7 ◯ lack ◯ late ◯ lake	8 ◯ pine ◯ pie ◯ pane	9 ◯ bet ◯ beat ◯ boat

Underline all the words that have a long vowel sound. Then circle **Yes** or **No** to answer each question.

10. Is a jeep the same as a jet?	Yes	No
11. Can a goat paint a gate?	Yes	No
12. Can a seal swim in the sea?	Yes	No
13. Is a peach a fruit?	Yes	No
14. Is a cape a big cap?	Yes	No
15. Can you hide a flute in a lime?	Yes	No
16. Is a dime the same as a vine?	Yes	No
17. Can you eat ice cream in a cone?	Yes	No

PHONICS Alive at Home — Review this Check-Up with your child.

CITY STREET

Honk—honk—honk!
Beep—beep—beep!
Hear the noise
Of city street.

Cars race fast,
Trucks bump past;
Creeping slow
The buses go.

Green turns red,
A sudden stop;
Up the hand
Of traffic cop.

Whistle shrill—
All is still;
Sudden hush—
The people rush.

Red turns green,
Then on again;
Cars race fast,
Trucks bump past.

Lois Lenski

Critical Thinking

How is the place where you live like this busy city? How is it different?

Name ______________________________

Dear Family,

As your child progresses through this unit about cities, she or he will learn about the two sounds of **c** and **g** and about consonant blends. A **consonant blend** is two or three consonants sounded together in a word so that each letter is heard.

- Read the words below with your child. Listen to the sounds of the letters that are underlined.

Apreciada Familia:

En esta unidad, sobre las ciudades, su niño aprenderá los dos sonidos de las letras **c** y **g** y la combinación de sonidos de las consonantes. Una **combinación de sonidos** se forma cuando dos o más consonantes están juntas pero cada una tiene su propio sonido al pronunciar la palabra.

- Lean las siguientes palabras. Escuchen el sonido de las letras subrayadas.

Hard c	Soft c
car	city

Hard g	Soft g
go	gym

Consonant Blends	
play	rent

- Read the poem "City Street" on the reverse side. Talk about the city scene.
- Help your child find words in the poem that sound like what they mean, for example: **honk, beep, bump.**
- Point out the consonant sounds in these words from the poem: soft **c** (city, race); hard **c** (cars, cop); hard **g** (go); consonant blends (honk, street, fast, trucks, bump, creeping, slow, green, stop, hand, traffic).

- Lean la poesía "City Street" en la página 83. Hablen de la escena en la ciudad.
- Ayude al niño a encontrar palabras cuyo sonido se parezca a su significado, por ejemplo: **honk, beep, bump.**
- Señale los sonidos de las consonantes en estas palabras de la poesía: **c** suave (city, race); **c** fuerte (cars, cop); **g** fuerte (go); combinación de consonantes (honk, street, fast, trucks, bump, creeping, slow, green, stop, hand, traffic).

PROJECT

Make a city skyscraper with your child. Use index cards or pieces of paper for the bricks. When your child learns a new word with hard or soft **c** or **g** or with a consonant blend, have him or her write the word on a brick and add it to the building.

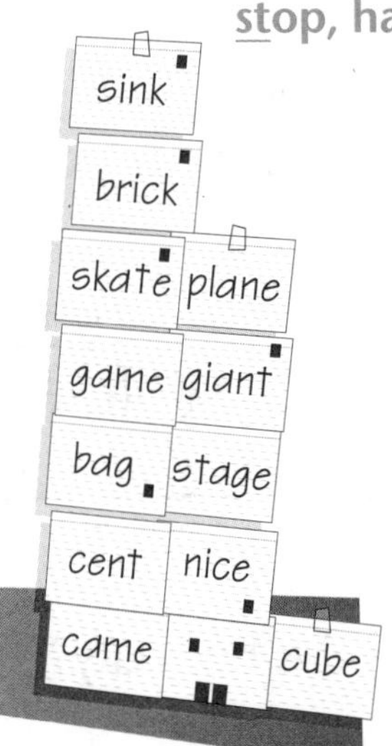

PROYECTO

Junto con el niño hagan un rascacielos. Use tarjetas 3X5 o pedazos de papel para los ladrillos. Cuando el niño aprenda una palabra nueva con sonido suave o fuerte de la **c** o la **g**, o de combinación, pídale escribirla en un ladrillo y pegarlo al edificio.

Name ______________________________

Car has the hard **c** sound. **City** has the soft **c** sound. Listen for the sounds of hard and soft **c** in the rhyme.

The cars in the city
Are all in a race.
Congratulations! You win!
You get a parking space.

Helpful Hint

C usually has the soft sound when it is followed by **e, i,** or **y.**

Say the name of each picture. Circle **Hard c** if the word has the hard **c** sound. Circle **Soft c** if it has the soft **c** sound.

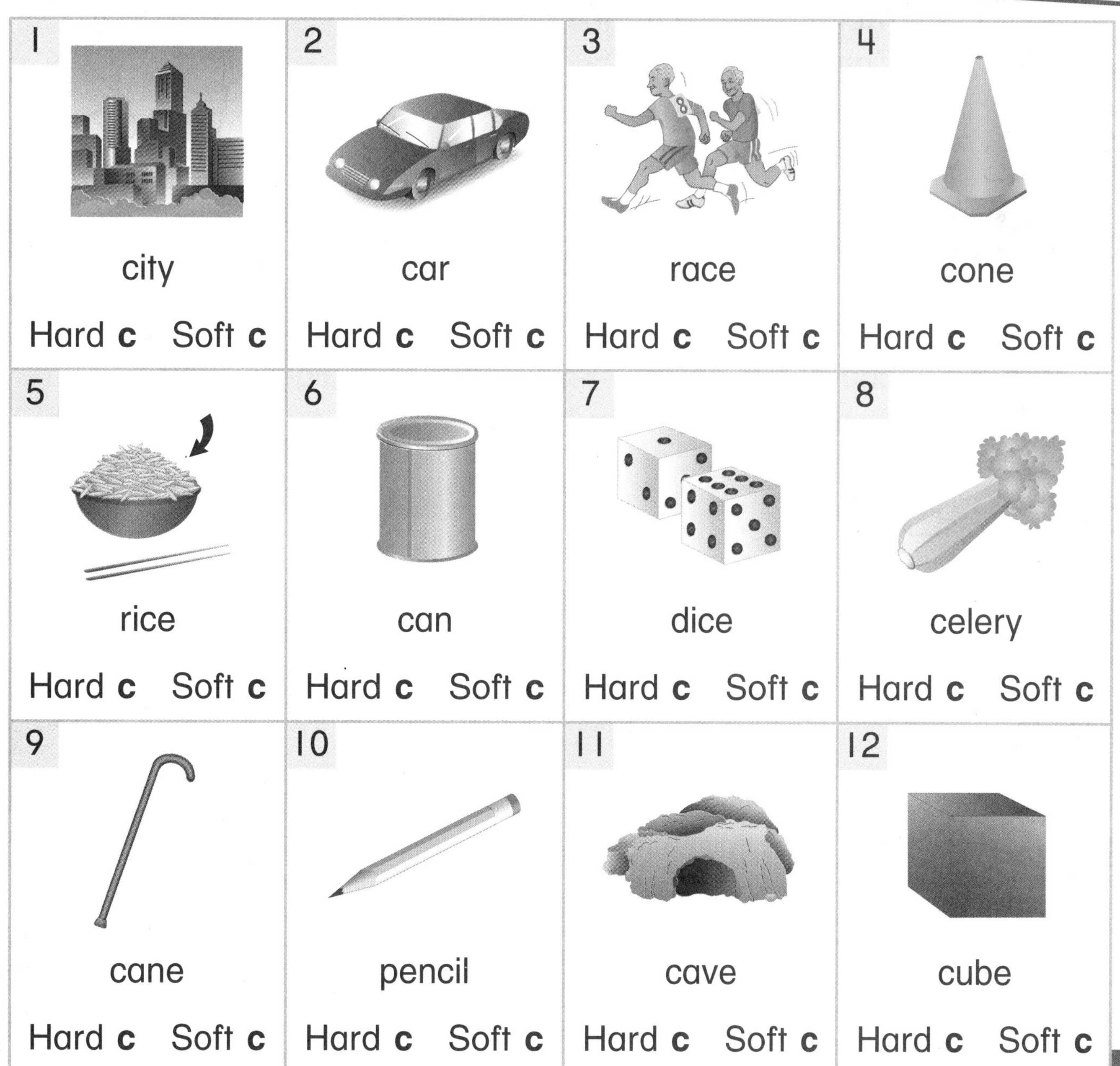

1	2	3	4
city	car	race	cone
Hard **c** Soft **c**	Hard **c** Soft **c**	Hard **c** Soft **c**	Hard **c** Soft **c**
5	6	7	8
rice	can	dice	celery
Hard **c** Soft **c**	Hard **c** Soft **c**	Hard **c** Soft **c**	Hard **c** Soft **c**
9	10	11	12
cane	pencil	cave	cube
Hard **c** Soft **c**	Hard **c** Soft **c**	Hard **c** Soft **c**	Hard **c** Soft **c**

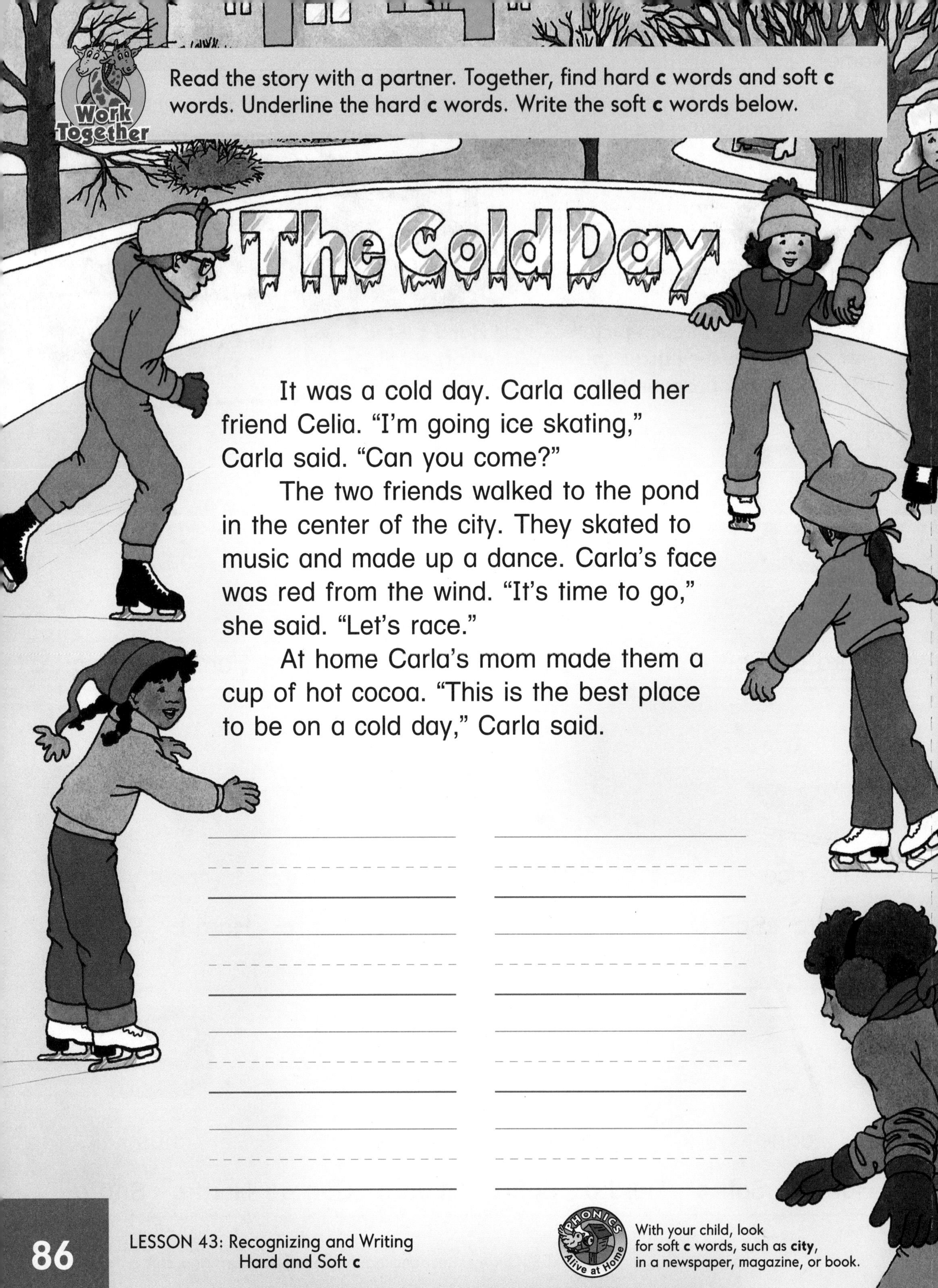

Work Together

Read the story with a partner. Together, find hard **c** words and soft **c** words. Underline the hard **c** words. Write the soft **c** words below.

The Cold Day

It was a cold day. Carla called her friend Celia. "I'm going ice skating," Carla said. "Can you come?"

The two friends walked to the pond in the center of the city. They skated to music and made up a dance. Carla's face was red from the wind. "It's time to go," she said. "Let's race."

At home Carla's mom made them a cup of hot cocoa. "This is the best place to be on a cold day," Carla said.

PHONICS Alive at Home

With your child, look for soft **c** words, such as **city**, in a newspaper, magazine, or book.

Name ________________________________

Games has the hard **g** sound. **Giant** has the soft **g** sound. Listen for the sounds of hard and soft **g** in the rhyme.

Our giant garage
Holds games and guitars,
Garbage bags, cages,
Gee—no room for cars!

Helpful Hint

G usually has the soft sound when it is followed by **e, i,** or **y.**

Say the name of each picture. Circle **Hard g** if the word has the hard **g** sound. Circle **Soft g** if it has the soft **g** sound.

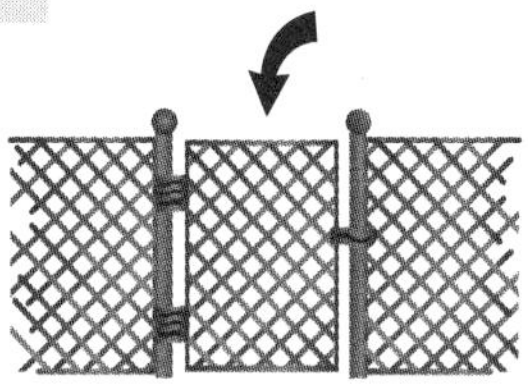

1	2	3	4
stage	gate	gem	goat
Hard **g** Soft **g**	Hard **g** Soft **g**	Hard **g** Soft **g**	Hard **g** Soft **g**
5	6	7	8
gym	bag	giant	giraffe
Hard **g** Soft **g**	Hard **g** Soft **g**	Hard **g** Soft **g**	Hard **g** Soft **g**
9	10	11	12
wagon	gum	gas	cage
Hard **g** Soft **g**	Hard **g** Soft **g**	Hard **g** Soft **g**	Hard **g** Soft **g**

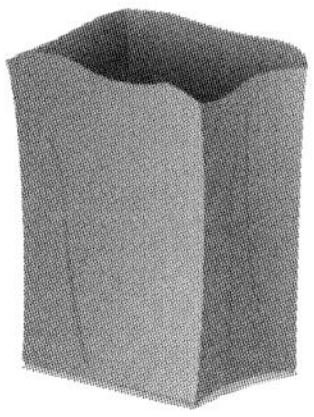

Read the movie titles on the posters. Underline the hard **g** words. Write the soft **g** words.

Make a movie poster. Write the title of a make-believe movie and draw a picture to go with it. In the title, use one hard **g** word and one soft **g** word.

Ask your child to read the soft **g** words he or she wrote and to name the letter that follows the soft **g** in each word.

Name ______________________________

Complete each line of the poem by writing a word from the box.
Read the poem and circle all of the hard **c** and **g** words.

car	game	gym	laces	page	space

City Games

Cindy has a friend who came ______________

To join her in a jumping ______________ .

Ed and Cal, who run in races, ______________

Always stop to tie their ______________ .

Gail and Gene set up on stage ______________

And take their turns to read a ______________ .

Look at the smile on Cam's face ______________

As she hops from space to ______________ .

Curt calls up his best pal Kim ______________

To shoot some baskets at the ______________ .

Now on his bike Miguel goes far. ______________

When he grows up, he'll drive a ______________ .

Circle the words in each list that have the same **c** or **g** sound as the picture name.

1	2	3	4
Hard **c**	Soft **c**	Hard **g**	Soft **g**
cane	nice	goal	bag
place	can	wagon	magic
cold	come	giant	giraffe
cup	dance	gem	goat

Write **H** beside each word that has the sound of hard **c** or **g**. Write **S** beside each word that has the sound of soft **c** or **g**.

5 cup ____	6 center ____	7 page ____	8 gate ____
9 gull ____	10 face ____	11 ice ____	12 car ____
13 gym ____	14 cage ____	15 gas ____	16 cube ____
17 race ____	18 fence ____	19 game ____	20 gentle ____

PHONICS Alive at Home Review this Check-Up with your child.

Name ______________________________

Block begins with the **l**-blend **bl.** Listen for the sounds of **l**-blends in the rhyme.

My block has a clock
Plus a flag and a slide.
Please come to my block.
We'll play and we'll glide.

Helpful Hint

A **consonant blend** is two or three consonants sounded together in a word so that each letter is heard.

Circle the **l**-blend that begins the name of each picture.

1	2	3	4
gl pl sl	gl pl fl	sl pl bl	bl cl fl

5	6	7	8
cl fl sl	sl gl bl	bl cl gl	bl sl pl

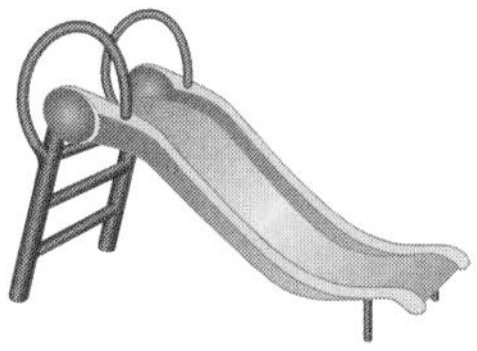

9	10	11	12
bl cl pl	pl sl fl	bl cl gl	fl gl bl

Write a sentence about something you see on a city block. Use a word with an **l**-blend. For example, "I see a bank with two big **cl**ocks."

Read the name of each picture. Then write a word with the same phonogram. Begin the new word with an **l**-blend from the box.

bl	cl	fl	gl	pl	sl

1	2	3
dad	**s**ock	**h**am
4	5	6
hay	**h**ide	**g**oat

Circle and write the word that completes the sentence. Read each sentence and have a partner say the **l**-blend word.

7. I'm ______________ to see you. glide glad

8. Let's go ______________ in the park. play clay

9. It's just two ______________ away. clocks blocks

10. We can try the new ______________. slide slam

Ask your child to read two **l**-blend words he or she wrote and to make up a sentence using both words.

Name ______________________________

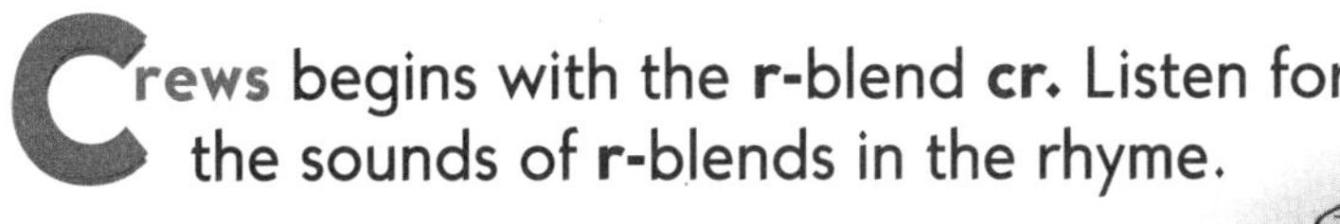

Crews begins with the **r**-blend **cr.** Listen for the sounds of **r**-blends in the rhyme.

Crews, fix the freeway!
Trucks, bring the gravel!
Now press quickly!
Drivers want to travel!

Helpful Hint

A **consonant blend** is two or three consonants sounded together in a word so that each letter is heard.

Say the name of each picture. Add an **r**-blend to the phonogram to write the picture name.

br	**cr**	**dr**	**fr**	**gr**	**pr**	**tr**

1 ____ain	2 ____um	3 ____ow	4 ____ick
5 ____een	6 ____ize	7 ____ame	8 ____ill
9 ____ee	10 ____ide	11 ____og	12 ____ab

Read the name of each picture. Then write a word with the same phonogram. Begin the new word with an **r**-blend from the box.

br	cr	fr	gr	pr	tr

1 **h**ill

2 **b**ee

3 **t**eam

4 **l**ake

5 **h**ide

6 **c**ape

Use a word from the box to complete each phrase.

cream	drill	frame	grape	prize	tree

7. drink ______ juice

8. eat ice ______

9. win a ______

10. get a picture ______

11. ______ a hole

12. plant a ______

PHONICS Alive at Home

With your child, take turns saying words that begin with **br, cr, dr, fr, gr, pr,** or **tr.**

Name ______________________________

Swing begins with the **s**-blend **sw.** Listen for the sounds of **s**-blends in the rhyme.

We play baseball on my street.
Swing that bat.
Smack that ball.
Now start running. Move those feet!

Helpful Hint

A **consonant blend** is two or three consonants sounded together in a word so that each letter is heard.

Circle the picture if its name begins with the same **s**-blend as the first picture in the row. Write the blend.

1  **st**amp	 ______	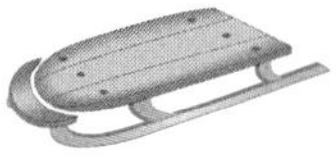 ______	 ______
2  **sw**ing	 ______	 ______	______
3 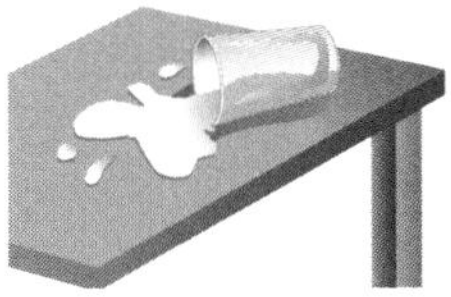 **sp**ill	 ______	 ______	______
4  **sk**ate	 ______	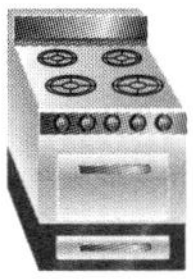 ______	 ______

Write a word with an **s**-blend to answer each question. Then take turns with a partner asking and answering the questions.

sc	sm	sn	squ	spr

1. What tells your weight and rhymes with **tale**? ______
2. What mouse sound rhymes with **beak**? ______
3. What crawls in the grass and rhymes with **rake**? ______
4. What means "not large" and rhymes with **tall**? ______
5. What comes each year and rhymes with **wing**? ______

Circle and write an **s**-blend to complete the word in each sentence.

6. A big truck sweeps the city ______eet. **str** **sw** **sl**
7. Brushes ______ub the street clean. **sc** **scr** **sn**
8. The truck also ______ays water. **st** **spr** **spl**
9. Watch out for the ______ash! **sl** **sp** **spl**

PHONICS Alive at Home

Together, make up rhyming questions like the ones at the top of the page for the words **street, scrub,** and **splash.**

Name ______________________________

Lift ends with the consonant blend **ft**. Listen for the sounds of final consonant blends in the rhyme.

Lift the last plank.
Don't let it bump or tilt!
Hold it still. I'll bolt it.
Now look what we have built!

Helpful Hint

A **consonant blend** is two or three consonants sounded together in a word so that each letter is heard.

Circle the blend that ends the name of each picture.

1	2	3	4
lf lt st	ft lf ld	nt nd nk	ft lt st

5	6	7	8
nk nd ld	mp nt st	lf nt mp	ft ld st

9	10	11	12
nd mp nk	st lt nt	lf lt ft	nd nk mp

Read each word. Then write a word with the same final blend.

1 ve**st**	2 bu**mp**	3 me**lt**	4 li**ft**
5 co**ld**	6 we**nt**	7 be**nd**	8 bu**nk**
9 sta**mp**	10 dri**nk**	11 sta**nd**	12 twi**st**

Use a word from the box to complete each sentence.

stand	went	best	drink

13. Last week, Mom and I ______________ to a street fair.

14. First we stopped at a fresh fruit ______________.

15. Then we got grape juice to ______________.

16. We had the ______________ time together!

Ask your child to read each word he or she wrote and circle the final blend (the last two letters).

Name ____________________

Look at the picture and read the word. Change the blend to write the word that names the picture.

1 **pr**ide	2 **gl**ue	3 **dr**ain
4 **sn**ow	5 **pl**ate	6 **sw**ing
7 **sm**og	8 **sp**ill	9 **br**ing
10 **sc**at	11 **gr**een	12 **cl**amp

Write the name of each picture in the puzzle. Then read down to find the answer to the question.

1 f i s t

2 ___ ___ ___ ___

3 ___ ___ ___ ___

4 ___ ___ ___ ___ ___

5 ___ ___ ___ ___

6 ___ ___ ___ ___

7 ___ ___ ___ ___ ___

8 ___ ___ ___ ___

9 ___ ___ ___ ___

10 ___ ___ ___ ___

What are two consonants sounded together at the end of a word?

a ______________ ______________

Ask your child to read a word he or she wrote and then say a word that ends with the same two letters: **fist**/**last.**

Name ______________________________

Use a word from the box to complete each sentence. Then practice reading the sentences aloud.

always	best	buy	their	us	work

1. Walk down Green Street with __________.

2. Dad and I will stop to __________ a stamp.

3. We might see Glen and Paige on their way to __________.

4. We might see Kim and Grant with __________ dog.

5. Kim and Grant __________ play with us.

6. Green Street is the __________ place!

Use one or more words from the box to answer the questions.

7. What are some things you might buy on a city street?

____

8. What do you think is the best place?

____

Read the letter. Then answer the questions.

Dear Grandpa,

Today we drove to see the cliffs in Colorado. Long ago, Native Americans made their homes in the cliffs. One huge cliff house is called Cliff Palace. Up to 400 people lived there! It had over 200 rooms. That's more than in my apartment building.

My building has four floors. Parts of Cliff Palace also have four floors. But I use stairs to climb up and down the floors. The people in Cliff Palace used ladders.

I'm glad we went to Cliff Palace. But I still like my apartment building the best!

Love and hugs,

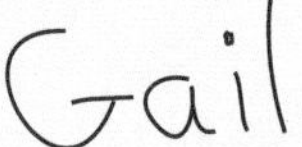

1. What is one way Cliff Palace is the same as an apartment building?

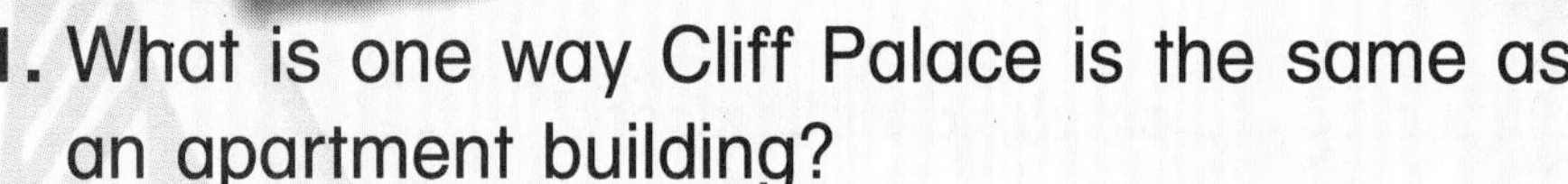

2. What is one way Cliff Palace is different from an apartment building?

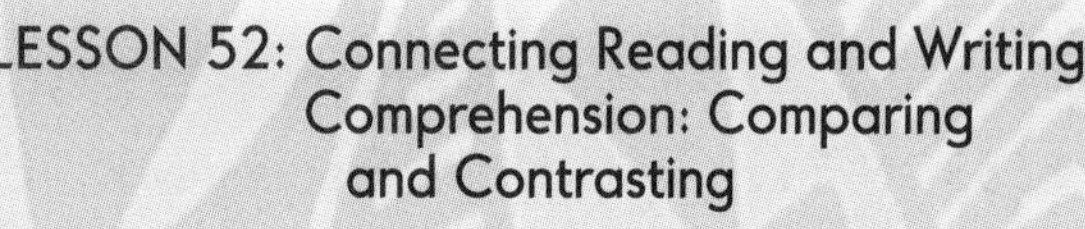

LESSON 52: Connecting Reading and Writing
Comprehension: Comparing and Contrasting

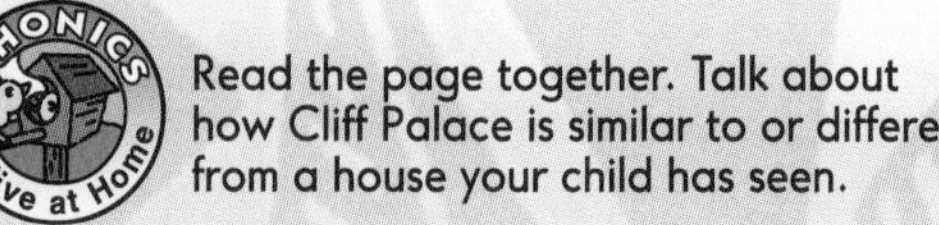

Read the page together. Talk about how Cliff Palace is similar to or different from a house your child has seen.

Name ____

Say, spell, and talk about each word in the box. Then write each word under the blend in its name.

train
glue
jump
flag
space
green
help
stage
play
fast
from
squeak

1 **l-**blend	2 **r-**blend
______	______
______	______
______	______
3 **s-**blend	4 Final Blend
______	______
______	______
______	______

Plan the scenery and sound effects for a play called "City Streets." Write what you will see and hear on the stage. Use two or more of your spelling words. Then read your descriptions to the class.

train	glue	jump	flag	space	green
help	stage	play	fast	from	squeak

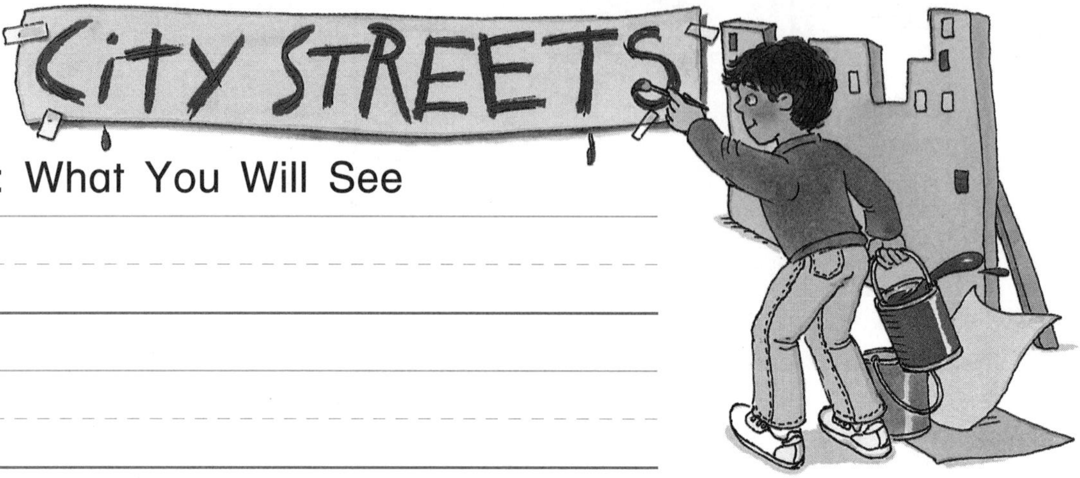

CITY STREETS

Scenery: What You Will See

Sound Effects: What You Will Hear

With your child, write sentences about your neighborhood using some of the spelling words in the box.

Name ____________________

Look and Learn

Let's read and talk about city streets.

The buildings are tall. They look like giants in the sky. The people look small as they hurry off to work. The sidewalks are always crowded. There's lots of noise. Cars move fast. Buses stop and go. Horns blow. Sirens scream. Brakes screech. City streets are busy places.

What do these pictures tell about the city? Tell how things look. Tell how things might sound.

Check-Up Fill in the circle next to the blend that begins the picture name.

1	2	3
○ pr ○ bl ○ pl	○ squ ○ str ○ spr	○ cr ○ cl ○ gr

4	5	6
○ sl ○ sk ○ cl	○ gr ○ cl ○ gl	○ sm ○ sn ○ sw

7	8	9
○ tr ○ str ○ dr	○ sl ○ st ○ sp	○ gr ○ dr ○ br

Circle the word that fits each clue.

10. You can run water in this.	sink	sift	wink
11. You can use this when you camp.	west	tent	test
12. You can find a bird in this.	vest	nest	bent
13. You can hold things in this.	hunk	damp	hand
14. You can put things in this.	trunk	tramp	sunk
15. You can put this on a desk.	last	land	lamp
16. You can give or get this.	sift	gust	gift
17. You can use this to hold up your pants.	belt	melt	best

PHONICS Alive at Home Review this Check-Up with your child.

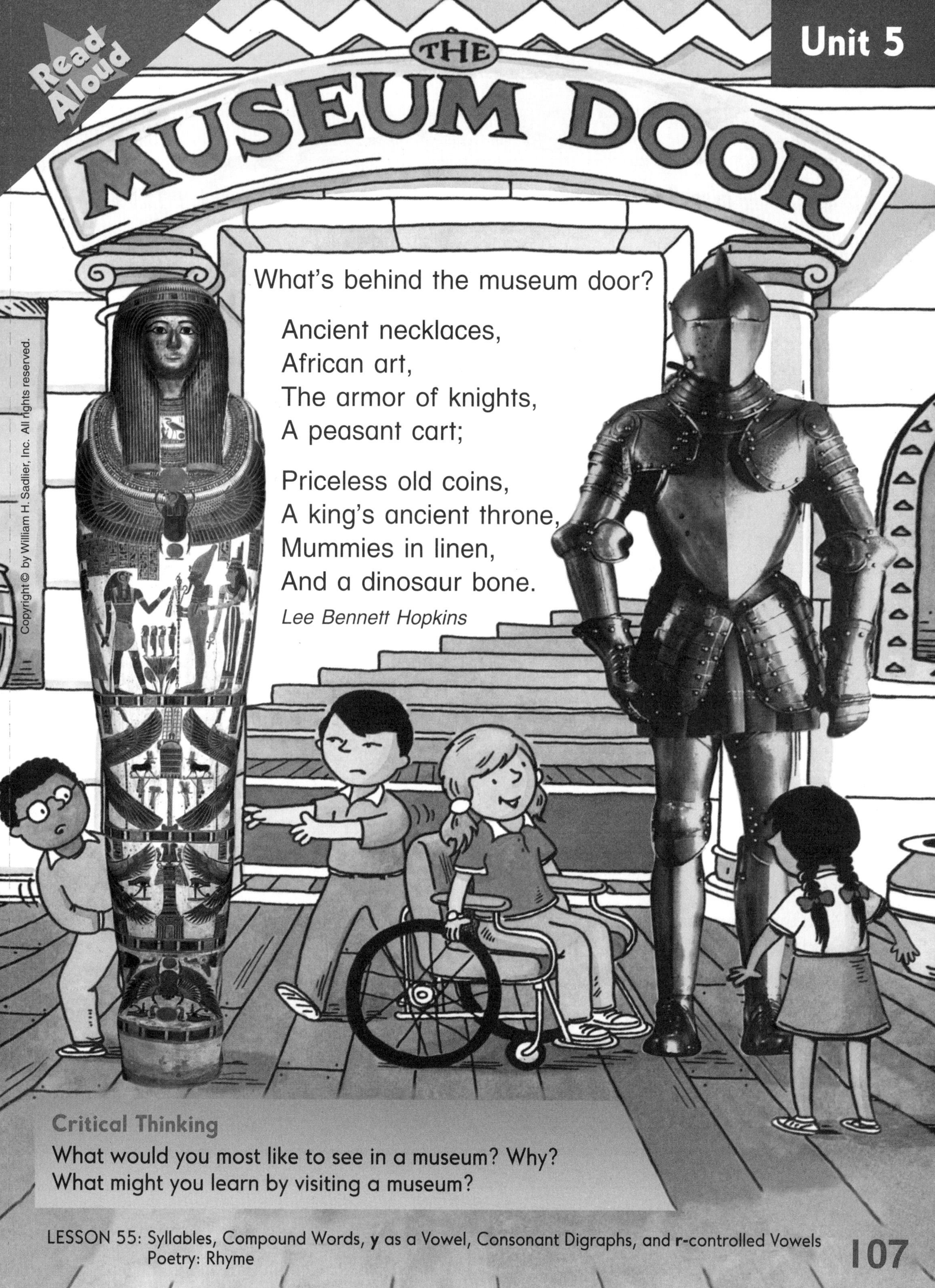

The Museum Door

What's behind the museum door?

Ancient necklaces,
African art,
The armor of knights,
A peasant cart;

Priceless old coins,
A king's ancient throne,
Mummies in linen,
And a dinosaur bone.

Lee Bennett Hopkins

Critical Thinking

What would you most like to see in a museum? Why?
What might you learn by visiting a museum?

LESSON 55: Syllables, Compound Words, **y** as a Vowel, Consonant Digraphs, and **r**-controlled Vowels
Poetry: Rhyme

Name ______________________________

Dear Family,

As your child progresses through this unit about going places, he or she will learn more about the following:

syllable: word or word part with one vowel sound; words can have one or more syllables (**wagon**: two vowel sounds = two syllables)

compound word: word made up of two or more smaller words (**raincoat**)

words with y as a vowel: words in which **y** has the sound of long **i** or long **e** (**fly, city**)

words ending in le: **apple**

consonant digraph: two consonants together that stand for one sound (**chin, tooth**)

words with ar, or, er, ir, ur: words in which **r** gives the vowel a new sound (**barn, corn, fern, bird, turn**)

- Read the poem "The Museum Door" on the reverse side. Talk about interesting places you and your child have visited.
- Read the poem again. Invite your child to read the lines that rhyme.

PROJECT

With your child, make a map of an imaginary town. As your child learns new words in this unit, use them to make up place names for the map. Help your child label the map.

Apreciada Familia:

En esta unidad, acerca de los paseos, su niño continuará aprendiendo sobre:

sílaba: pálabra o parte de una palabra que tiene un sonido vocal; las palabras pueden tener una o más sílabas (**wagon**: dos sonidos vocales = dos sílabas)

palabras compuestas: aquellas formadas por dos o más palabras (**raincoat**)

y con sonido de vocal: palabras en las que la **y** tiene el sonido largo de la **i** o la **e** (**fly, city**)

palabras que terminan en le: **apple**

consonantes dígrafas: dos consonantes juntas que producen un solo sonido (**chin, tooth**)

palabras con ar, or, er, ir, ur: palabras donde la letra **r** da a la vocal un nuevo sonido (**barn, corn, fern, bird, turn**)

- Lea la poesía "The Museum Door" en la página 107. Hablen de los otros lugares interesantes que hayan visitado.
- Lea el poema de nuevo. Invite a su niño a leer los versos que riman.

PROYECTO

Dibujen el mapa de un pueblo imaginario el cual le gustaría visitar. Con las palabras aprendidas en esta unidad busquen nombres para el mapa. Ayude al niño a rotular el mapa.

Name ______________________________

The word **sea** has one syllable. The word **visit** has two syllables. Listen for one- and two-syllable words in the rhyme.

Someday I'll visit
The bottom of the sea.
Won't you come along?
Just think what we will see!

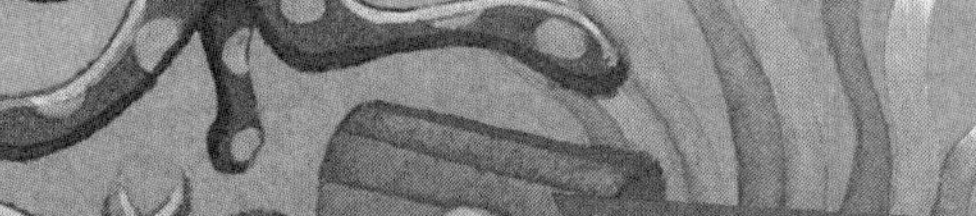

Helpful Hint

A **syllable** is a word or word part with one vowel sound. Words can have one or more syllables.

Say the name of each picture. Listen for the vowel sounds. Write **1** or **2** for the number of vowel sounds, or syllables, you hear.

1 	2	3	4
2			
5 	**6** 	**7** 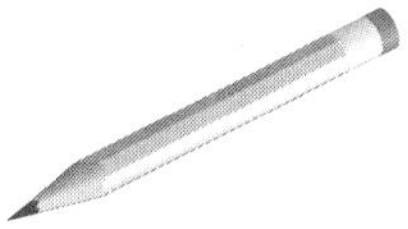	**8** 
9 	**10** 	**11** 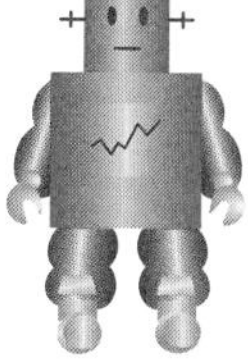	**12** 

Work Together

What's behind the museum door? Color the things that have two syllables in their name. Then write two sentences to describe your favorite one. Read your sentences to a partner.

LESSON 56: Recognizing and Writing Two-Syllable Words

PHONICS Alive at Home

Ask your child to find objects in your home that have two-syllable names, such as **window, table,** or **sofa.**

Name ______________________________

The compound word **spaceship** is made by combining the words **space** and **ship.** Listen and look for compound words in the rhyme.

Spaceship countdown,
Blastoff this afternoon!
Tonight we'll see starlight
And walk on the moon!

Helpful Hint

A **compound word** is made up of two or more smaller words.

Combine a word from Box 1 with a word from Box 2 to name each picture. Write the compound word.

Box 1		
back	pea	rain
base	play	star
mail	pop	wind

Box 2		
ball	corn	nut
bow	fish	pack
box	mill	pen

1 ______	2 ______	3 ______
4 ______	5 ______	6 ______
7 ______	8 ______	9 ______

Combine each word with the name of the picture and write the compound word. Then say the word. Write the number of syllables you hear.

1. ant ______ ☐

2. cake ______ ☐

3. set ______ ☐

Make compound words. Draw a line from each word in the first column to a word in the second column. Then answer the question below.

4	rain	side	12	day	weed
5	week	cup	13	sea	dream
6	tea	coat	14	suit	fruit
7	in	end	15	grape	case
8	her	boat	16	air	flake
9	tree	self	17	bee	way
10	row	box	18	snow	hive
11	sand	top	19	run	port

20. How many syllables are in each compound word that you made? ☐

Pretend you discovered a new planet. Make up a compound word for the planet's name. Write a sentence or two to describe your planet.

PHONICS Alive at Home

Ask your child to hold up two fingers each time you say a compound word: **sunrise, moon, nighttime, rainbow, star.**

Name ____________________

The **y** in **fly** has the long **i** sound. The **y** in **dizzy** has the long **e** sound. Listen for the sounds of **y** in the rhyme.

"Fly, why are you dizzy?
Tell us if you can."
"My!" said Fly. "That's easy.
I'm spinning on a fan."

Helpful Hint

Sometimes **y** has the sound of long **i.** Sometimes **y** has the sound of long **e.**

Say the name of each picture. Circle **Long i** if the **y** has the long **i** sound. Circle **Long e** if it has the long **e** sound.

1	2	3	4
fly	city	penny	cry
Long **i** Long **e**	Long **i** Long **e**	Long **i** Long **e**	Long **i** Long **e**
5	6	7	8
forty	sky	bunny	candy
Long **i** Long **e**	Long **i** Long **e**	Long **i** Long **e**	Long **i** Long **e**
9	10	11	12
daisy	dry	pony	twenty
Long **i** Long **e**	Long **i** Long **e**	Long **i** Long **e**	Long **i** Long **e**

Read each title in the video library. Write the words in which **y** has the sound of long **i** under the **fly.** Write the words in which **y** has the sound of long **e** under the **city.** Then say each word. Write the number of syllables you hear.

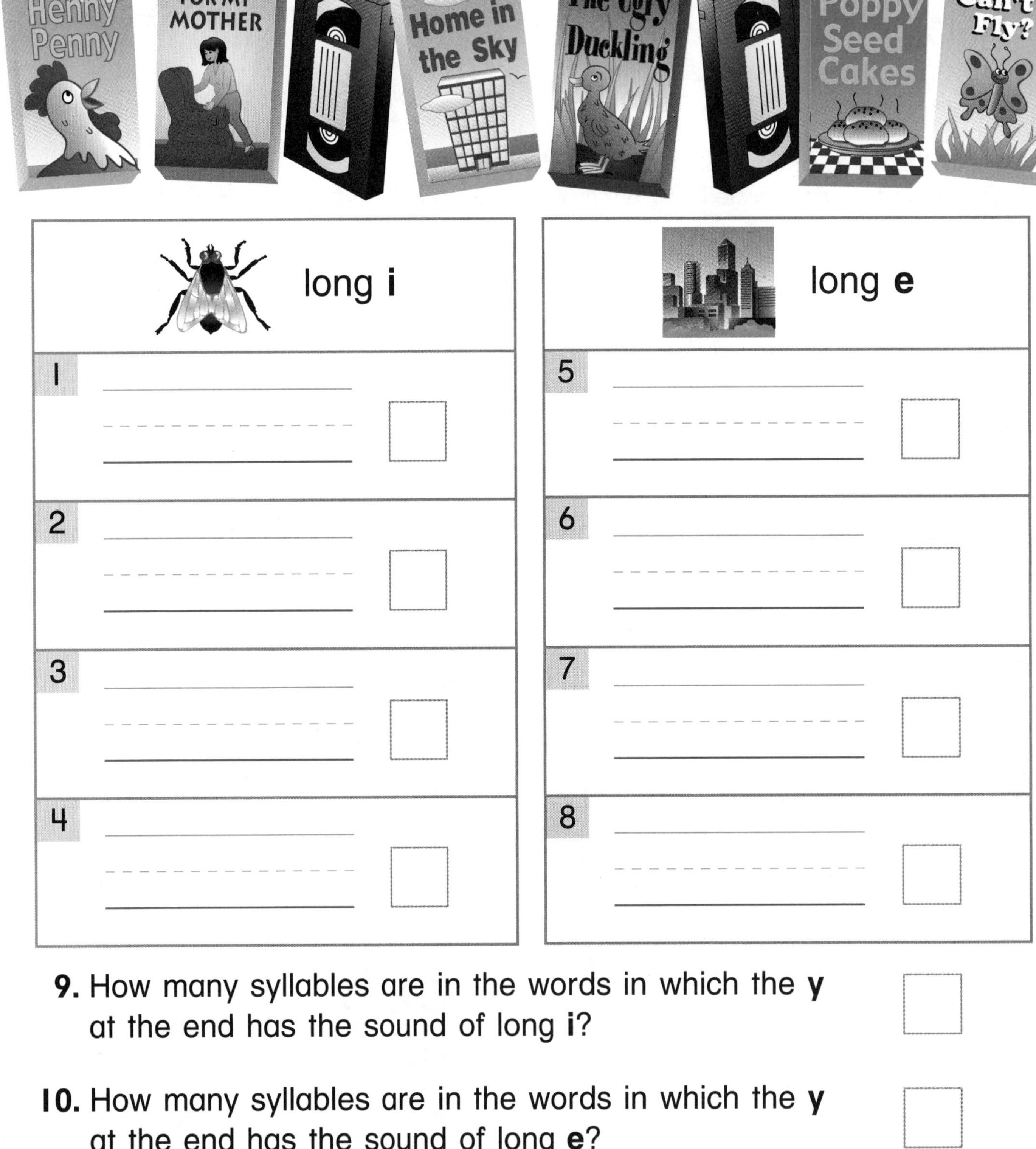

9. How many syllables are in the words in which the **y** at the end has the sound of long **i**?

10. How many syllables are in the words in which the **y** at the end has the sound of long **e**?

PHONICS Alive at Home

Say these words and ask your child how many syllables each has: **daisy, twenty, try, happy, shy, by.**

Name ________________________________

Eagle ends with the **le** sound. Listen for the sound of **le** in the rhyme.

An eagle and a turtle
Each took a little trip.
One flew in a circle.
One sailed a purple ship.

Helpful Hint

Some words end with the sound of **le**.

Find and write the word that names each picture.

ankle needle	apple pickle	bottle purple	candle rattle	circle table	eagle turtle

1 ______________	2 ______________
3 ______________	4 ______________
5 ______________	6 ______________
7 ______________	8 ______________
9 ______________	10 ______________
11 ______________	12 ______________

Circle the words in the box that end in **le.**

circle	crackle	feel	hope	juggle	light
little	people	puddle	purple	rattle	suit

Use an **le**-word from above to complete the sentence. Say the word and write the number of syllables you hear. Then answer the question.

1. Many ______________ go to the fair. ☐

2. We watch the clown ______________. ☐

3. We ride the ponies in a ______________. ☐

4. We see ______________ pigs in a pen. ☐

5. One pig plays in a ______________. ☐

6. How many syllables are in each **le**-word that you wrote? ☐

PHONICS Alive at Home

Draw a circle. Inside it, ask your child to write words that end in **le,** such as **puzzle** and **wiggle.**

Name ______________________________

Write the compound word from the box that fits each clue.

anthill	beanbag	beehive	rowboat	seaweed	snowflake

1. This is a boat you row. ____________
2. This is a hive for bees. ____________
3. This is a hill made by ants. ____________
4. This is a weed that grows in the sea. ____________
5. This is a flake of snow. ____________
6. This is a bag filled with beans. ____________

Write **i** beside each word in which **y** has the long **i** sound. Write **e** beside each word in which **y** has the long **e** sound.

7	8	9	10
fly ____	city ____	try ____	daisy ____
11	**12**	**13**	**14**
candy ____	penny ____	dry ____	why ____

Make compound words. Draw a line from each word in the first column to a word in the second column. Write the new word.

ant	cake
tree	hill
pea	ball
base	top
pan	nut

1 ____
2 ____
3 ____
4 ____
5 ____

her	bow
in	end
tea	self
rain	side
week	cup

6 ____
7 ____
8 ____
9 ____
10 ____

Circle the words in which **y** has the same sound as the picture name.

11

Long **i**

sky	by
bunny	city
penny	why
try	cry

12

Long **e**

dry	twenty
forty	ugly
pony	my
fly	candy

PHONICS Alive at Home Review this Check-Up with your child.

Name ______________________________

Cheerful begins with the consonant digraph **ch.** Listen for the sounds of consonant digraphs **th, sh, wh,** and **ch** in the rhyme.

The cheerful whale
Held her tail up high.
Then she sailed like a ship
As she called out good-bye.

Helpful Hint

A **consonant digraph** is two consonants together that stand for one sound.

Circle the consonant digraph that begins the name of each picture.

1	2	3
th sh wh	ch sh th	wh ch th
4	**5**	**6**
sh wh ch	th sh wh	ch th sh
7	**8**	**9**
wh sh th	sh wh ch	th ch wh
10	**11**	**12**
th sh ch	wh ch th	sh wh ch

Work with your classmates to list **thirteen** words that begin with consonant digraphs.

Circle and write the word that completes each sentence.

1. Do you know ______________ the president lives? where what

2. ______________ I give you a hint? Shall Chill

3. George Washington ______________ the place. chase chose

4. But he didn't have a ______________ to live there. change chance

5. It is painted ______________. white wheat

6. I ______________ it's a good place to visit. thing think

7. Let me ______________ you Washington, D.C. chow show

Work Together

Change the beginning digraph and write a rhyming word. Use **th, sh, wh,** or **ch.** Read your answers to a partner.

8 **ch**in	9 **ch**eep	10 **sh**op	11 **wh**ine
12 **sh**ip	13 **ch**eat	14 **wh**y	15 **th**ick

PHONICS Alive at Home

Ask your child to sort his or her answers from this page under the headings **th, sh, wh,** and **ch.**

Name ___________________________________

Jack ends with the consonant digraph **ck.** Listen for the sounds of final consonant digraphs **ck, th, sh,** and **ch** in the rhyme.

Jack and Beth
Both rush to the beach.
They fish with a stick
And snack on a peach.

Helpful Hint

A **consonant digraph** is two consonants together that stand for one sound.

Circle the consonant digraph that ends the name of each picture.

1	2	3
ck th sh	ch ck th	ch sh ck
4	**5**	**6**
th sh ch	ck th sh	ch ck th

Circle the word that fits each clue.

7. This has wheels.	rock	truck
8. This is sandy.	beach	peach
9. This holds food.	duck	dish
10. This shows the time.	clock	click
11. This swims in the sea.	wish	fish
12. These show when you smile.	teeth	teach

Use a word from the box to complete each sentence.

beach	both	fresh	peach	truck	with

1. I went on a trip ______________ my uncle.

2. We drove north in his ______________.

3. The truck was loaded with ______________ fish.

4. We drove by a sandy ______________.

5. At noon we ______________ ate a sandwich.

6. We each ate a ripe ______________, too.

Write a rhyming word.

7 wish	8 back	9 block
______	______	______
10 bath	**11 teach**	**12 booth**
______	______	______

LESSON 65: Writing Final Consonant Digraphs
ck, th, sh, ch

PHONICS Alive at Home

With your child, use the words at the top of the page to make up a story about a trip you would like to take.

Name ______________________

Knight begins with the consonant digraph **kn**. Listen for the sound of **kn** in the rhyme.

I'll buy the rusty knight
That has the knobby knees.
Pack him up quickly.
I'll take him with me, please.

Helpful Hint

A **consonant digraph** is two consonants together that stand for one sound.

Circle the word that names each picture.

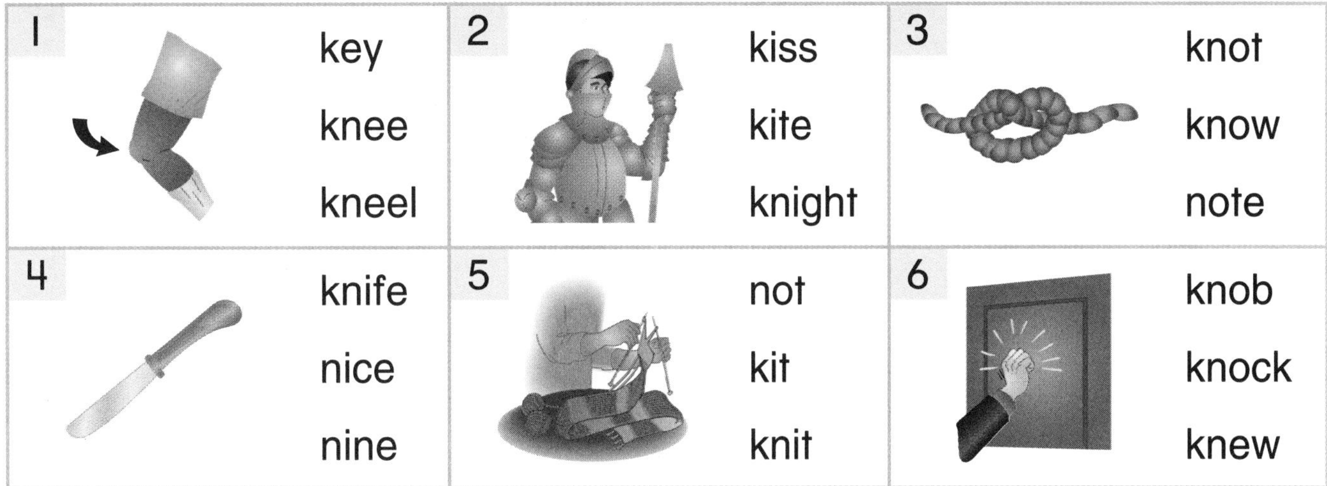

1	key knee kneel	2	kiss kite knight	3	knot know note
4	knife nice nine	5	not kit knit	6	knob knock knew

Fill in the circle next to the word that completes the sentence. Write the word in the sentence.

7. I ______________ a shop that sells all kinds of things. ○ know ○ knee

8. There is a ______________ in armor at the door. ○ knife ○ knight

9. Just ______________ and you can go inside. ○ knit ○ knock

10. You'll find brass ______________ for your door. ○ knobs ○ knots

Wrist begins with the consonant digraph **wr.** Listen for the sound of **wr** in the rhyme.

The watch on my wrist
Is wrong—it's slow.
No time to wrap gifts.
I'll just put on some bows.

Helpful Hint

A **consonant digraph** is two consonants together that stand for one sound.

Circle the word that names each picture.

1	2	3
rip wrist wish	which reach wrench	whip wrap ripe
4	**5**	**6**
write white wheat	read wreath with	rent went wren

Write a wr-word from above to complete each sentence.

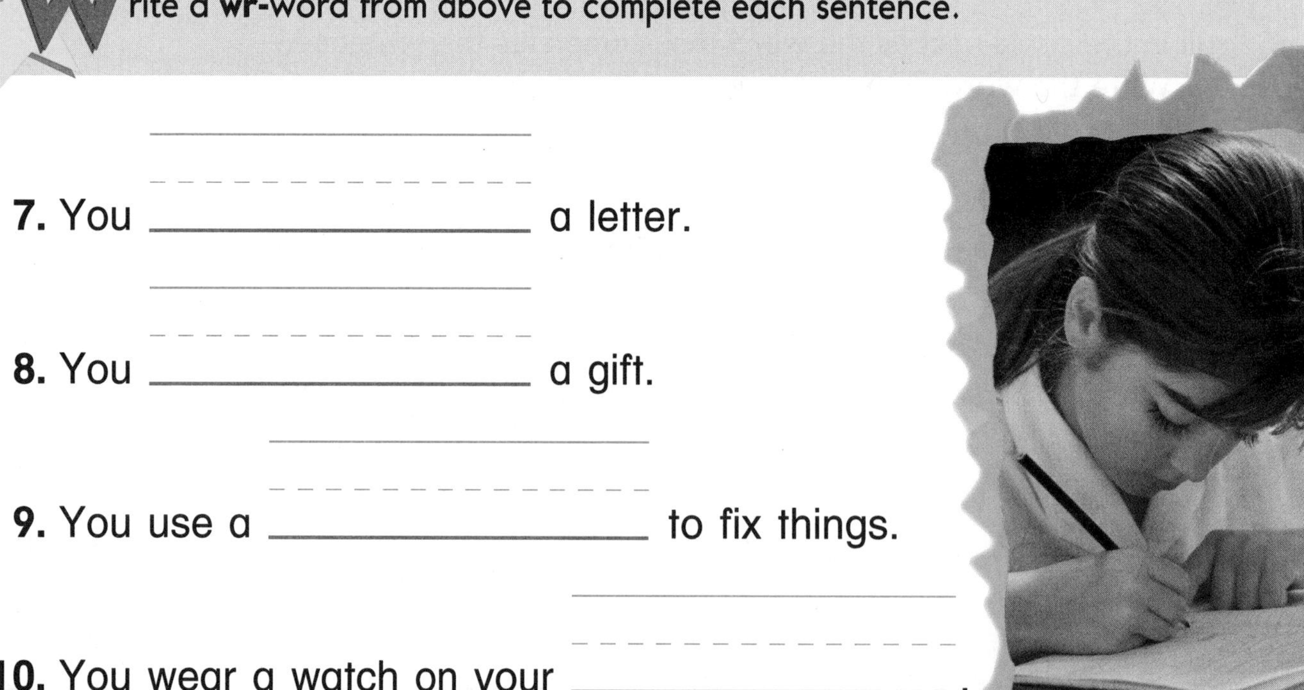

7. You ________________ a letter.

8. You ________________ a gift.

9. You use a ________________ to fix things.

10. You wear a watch on your ________________.

Ask your child to read the sentences he or she completed. Together, make up more sentences with these **wr**-words.

Name ____________________

Spell, Write, and Tell Say, spell, and talk about each word in the box. Then write each word under the digraph in its name. Circle the digraph in each word.

thorn
truck
chose
wrote
peach
why
knee
show
black
wash
both
what

1 th	2 sh	3 wh

4 ch	5 ck

6 kn	7 wr

WELCOME TO PEACH COUNTRY

Be a tour guide. Welcome a visitor to your favorite place and tell about it. Write what you would say. Use one or more of your spelling words. Then read your speech to the class.

thorn	truck	chose	wrote	peach	why
knee	show	black	wash	both	what

Welcome to

PHONICS Alive at Home — With your child, use one or more spelling words to describe a place in your neighborhood.

Name ______________________________

Look at the picture clues. Write the words in the puzzles.

DOWN

1

2

ACROSS

3

4

DOWN

5

6

ACROSS

7

8

Check-Up Circle the consonant digraph that **begins** each picture name.

1	2	3
th sh wh	wr ch wh	th kn wr

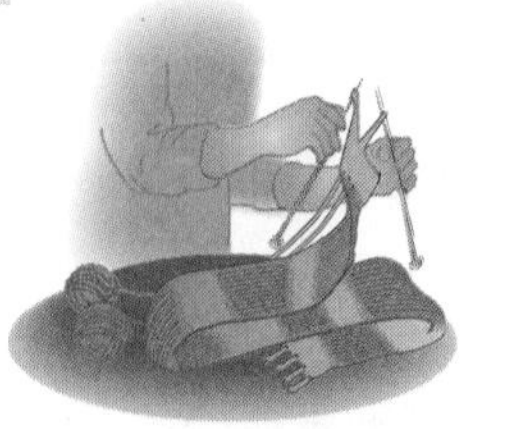

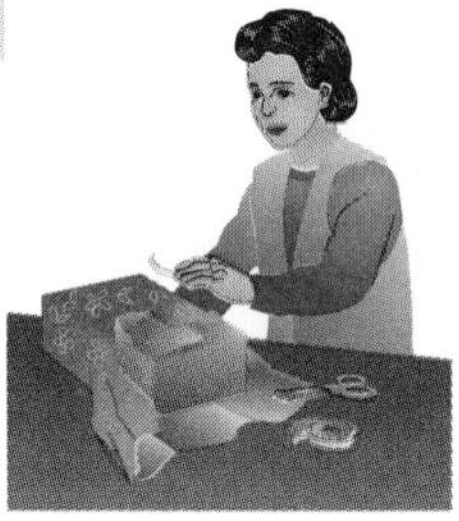

4	5	6
wr sh wh	sh kn ch	sh th ch

7	8	9
sh wh ch	th kn wh	wr sh wh

Circle the consonant digraph that **ends** each picture name.

10	11	12
th sh ch	ck th sh	th sh ch

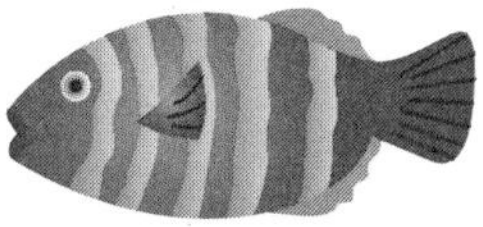

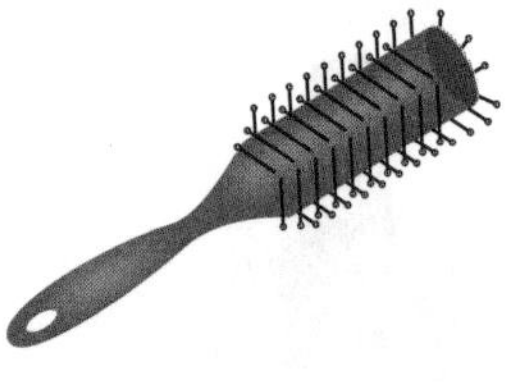

13	14	15
ck th ch	th sh ch	ck sh ch

Name ______________________________

Large has the **ar** sound. Listen for the sound of **ar** in the rhyme.

On a large red carpet
I can travel quite far.
I start on my farm
And park on a star.

Helpful Hint

An **r** after a vowel gives the vowel a new sound.

Circle and write the **ar**-word that names each picture.

1	2	3
bark barn bank	star tar stand	car cat cart
______	______	______
4	**5**	**6**
arm ark am	jam jack jar	hard part harp
______	______	______
7	**8**	**9**
dark date dart	yak yard yarn	garden carpet garment
______	______	______

With a partner, use a word from the box to complete each sentence.

bark	barn	dark	far	farm	hard

1. Is it ____________ to milk a cow?

2. Ask Mrs. Martin! She lives on a ____________.

3. It is not ____________ from my house.

4. There are many animals in the ____________.

5. Sparky the dog likes to ____________ at the cows.

6. Sometimes I visit until it gets ____________.

Write a rhyming word.

7 harm	8 star	9 yard
10 lark	11 yarn	12 dart

Draw a star. Inside it, ask your child to write **ar**-words, such as **park** and **car**.

Name ____________________

Forty has the **or** sound. Listen for the sound of **or** in the rhyme.

Forty-two horses went sailing
A long way from the shore.
A storm came down from the north.
Now they won't sail anymore.

Helpful Hint

An **r** after a vowel gives the vowel a new sound.

Find and write the **or**-word that names each picture.

forty	horn	core	horse	cork
corn	thorn	fork	torch	

1 ________	2 ________	3 ________
4 ________	5 ________	6 ________
7 ________	8 ________	9 40 ________

Fill in the circle next to the word that completes the sentence. Write the word in the sentence.

1. I am at a ______________ ranch.
   - ○ horse
   - ○ tore

2. My horse has a ______________ tail.
   - ○ horn
   - ○ short

3. I am riding in a ______________ field.
   - ○ corn
   - ○ fork

4. I won't go near that ______________ bush!
   - ○ thorn
   - ○ port

5. Look! A big ______________ is coming.
   - ○ cord
   - ○ storm

6. Oh no! I want ______________ time to ride!
   - ○ more
   - ○ torch

Work Together

Write a rhyming word. Compare answers with a partner. Are your words the same or different?

7 horn	8 form	9 store
______________	______________	______________
10 fort	**11 stork**	**12 porch**
______________	______________	______________

PHONICS Alive at Home: Make new words with your child by replacing the **ar** in these words with **or: card, barn, part, farm, stare.**

Name ______________________________

Perched has the **er** sound. The letters **ir** and **ur** can also make this sound. Listen for this sound in the rhyme.

Thirty birds hurried
To a mountain miles away.
They perched in fir trees
And chirped away the day.

Helpful Hint

An **r** after a vowel gives the vowel a new sound.

Sort the words. Write the **er**-words under **fern,** the **ir**-words under **bird,** and the **ur**-words under **purse.**

burn	dirt	first	girl	her	herd
nurse	perch	serve	thirty	turkey	turn

1 fern	2 bird	3 purse

Write a silly sentence with an **er**-word, an **ir**-word, and a **ur**-word. For example, "At the **turkey** farm, I saw **thirty birds** on one **perch.**"

Fill in the circle next to the word that completes the sentence. Write the word in the sentence.

1. Let's go to the ________________.
   - ○ circus
   - ○ curve

2. Mom has tickets in her ________________.
   - ○ chirp
   - ○ purse

3. Please ________________ or we'll be late.
   - ○ furry
   - ○ hurry

4. Mom will be ________________ in line.
   - ○ fir
   - ○ first

5. I'll stand next to ________________.
   - ○ her
   - ○ hurt

6. You will be ________________.
   - ○ third
   - ○ thirst

7. The clowns ________________ out of the car.
   - ○ stir
   - ○ burst

8. They ________________ and toss big hoops.
   - ○ twirl
   - ○ nerve

9. Now they ________________ water at each other.
   - ○ burn
   - ○ squirt

10. When can I have a ________________?
   - ○ turn
   - ○ term

PHONICS Alive at Home

Ask your child to sort his or her answers from this page under the headings **er**-words, **ir**-words, and **ur**-words.

Name ____

Draw a line from each word in the first column to a rhyming word in the second column.

1	park	tar	9	farm	worn
2	scar	porch	10	form	charm
3	sore	spark	11	born	yarn
4	torch	more	12	barn	storm
5	dark	thorn	13	start	mark
6	arm	shore	14	pork	stork
7	score	harm	15	short	smart
8	torn	bark	16	shark	sport

Circle all the **ar**-words. Underline all the **or**-words. Then circle **Yes** or **No** to answer each question.

17. Can a park path be short?	Yes	No
18. Can a horse play a harp?	Yes	No
19. Can you buy a scarf in a store?	Yes	No
20. Is a fork the same as a torch?	Yes	No
21. Can a shark throw darts?	Yes	No
22. Is an acorn made of yarn?	Yes	No
23. Can a stork play cards?	Yes	No
24. Can a dog bark and snarl?	Yes	No
25. Does corn have thorns?	Yes	No
26. Can you read a story in the morning?	Yes	No

A **nursery** is a place where plants are grown and sold. Look at the picture of the nursery. Then follow the directions below.

Directions

1. Circle the name of the nursery.
2. Make an X on the clerk.
3. Color the bird's perch brown.
4. Color the bird blue and yellow.
5. Draw a box around the turtle.
6. Color the turnip tops green.
7. Color the fir trees blue.
8. Draw some ferns in the dirt.
9. Color the girl's skirt purple.
10. Color the boy's T-shirt red.
11. Draw a star on the purse.
12. Draw a furry kitten anywhere.

With your child, make up a story about this scene using the words **nursery, bird, turtle, ferns, skirt,** and **purse.**

Name ______________________________

Ready to Read

Use a word from the box to complete each sentence.
Then practice reading the sentences aloud.

First	or	very	Which	Would	your

1. ______________ you like to take a trip?

2. ______________ we can drive to the beach and surf.

3. Then we can fly to a ______________ big city.

4. Last we can stop at a park ______________ a farm.

5. ______________ place would you like best?

6. Maybe the best place is ______________ backyard!

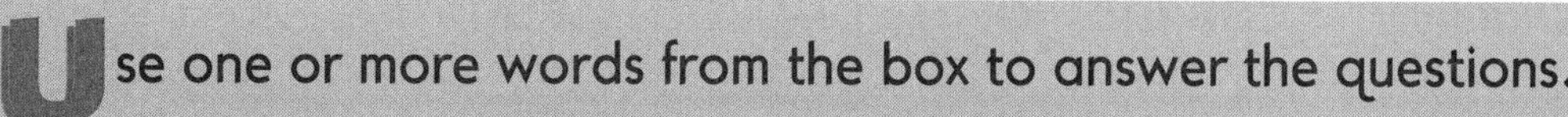

Use one or more words from the box to answer the questions.

7. What place would you like to visit?

____

8. What question would you ask a friend who had taken a trip?

____

Read the play. Then answer the questions.

Earth Visit
A Play in 3 Acts

Act One—Planet Knick-Knack

Chid-Chid: Let's take a trip in our spaceship.

Shub-Shub: We can fly to Earth for the weekend.

Whicky-Whacky: We will be there in thirteen hours.

Act Two—A Beach on Earth

Chid-Chid: First, let's swim like fish in the water.

Shub-Shub: Then we can try to surf!

Whicky-Whacky: Let's write a postcard and eat an Earth snack. Popcorn!

Act Three—Back on Planet Knick-Knack

Chid-Chid: I kept something to remember our visit—a pretty shell.

Shub-Shub: I kept this shiny penny.

Whicky-Whacky: I kept this jar of popcorn. Yummy!

1. What is one thing the space kids want to do at the beach?

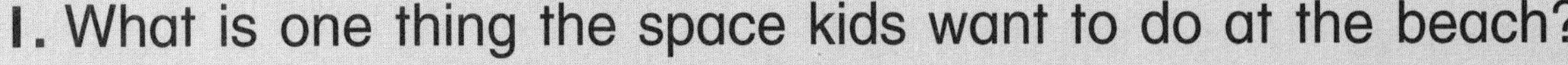

2. What would you like to do at the beach?

LESSON 74: Connecting Reading and Writing
Comprehension: Relating to Personal Experiences

Phonics Alive at Home: Read the play with your child. Ask: Where would you like to take a trip?

Name ______________________________

Spell, Write, and Tell

Say, spell, and talk about each word in the box. Then write each word under the correct heading.

before
clerk
far
first
girl
her
herd
horse
purse
start
store
turn

1 **er-**words

2 **or-**words

3 **ar-**words

4 **ir-**words

5 **ur-**words

Write a letter to a friend. Tell about a trip that you have taken or would like to take. Use one or more of your spelling words. Then share your letters.

before	first	herd	start
clerk	girl	horse	store
far	her	purse	turn

Dear ____________,

You'll never guess where I went!

Your friend,

Ask your child to read his or her letter to you and to name the **er**-words, **ir**-words, and **ur**-words.

Name ______________________________

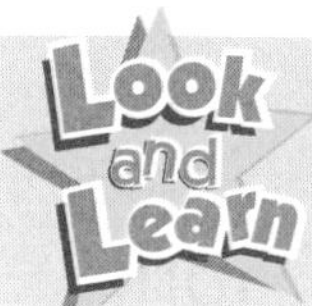

Look and Learn Let's read and talk about the Statue of Liberty.

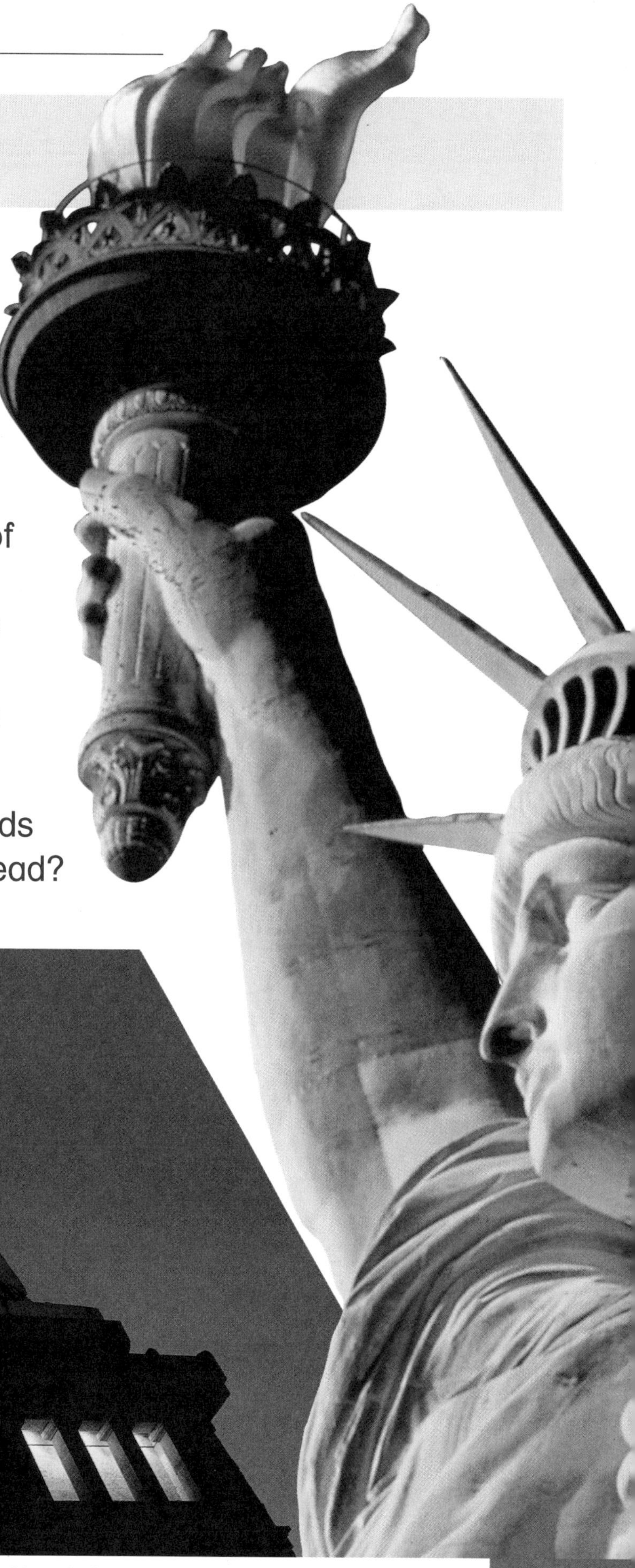

Meet Miss Liberty. That's what some people call this statue. Miss Liberty stands on an island in New York harbor. She greets people who come to the United States. Miss Liberty was a gift to us from the people of France. She's very tall. In fact, she's 152 feet high and stands on a base that's 150 feet high. Miss Liberty holds the torch of freedom above her head.

Why do you think Miss Liberty holds the torch of freedom above her head?

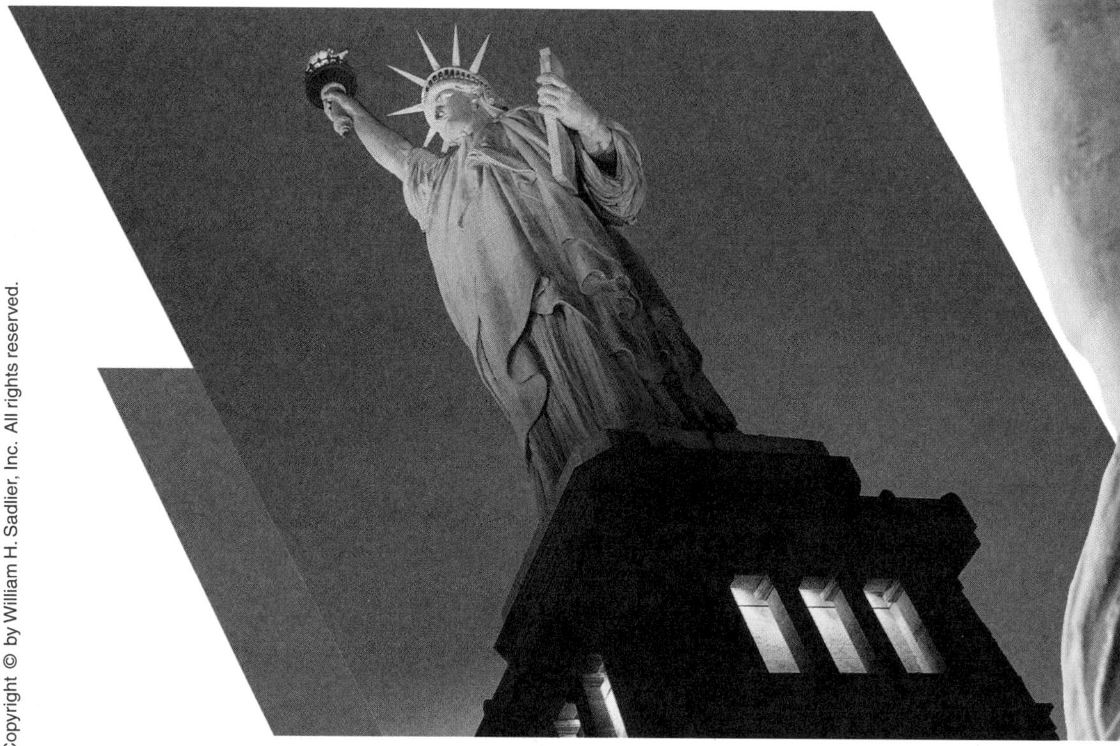

Check-Up Fill in the circle next to the word that names the picture.

1 ○ car ○ core ○ curb	2 ○ bark ○ bird ○ bore	3 ○ fork ○ far ○ fern
4 ○ barn ○ burn ○ born	5 ○ harp ○ horn ○ horse	6 ○ pork ○ perch ○ purse

Write the word from the box that fits each clue.

fork	her	large	perch	shirt	turn

7. This is where birds sit. ______________________

8. This goes with a knife. ______________________

9. This means the same as **big.** ______________________

10. This goes with your pants. ______________________

11. This means the same as **spin.** ______________________

12. This is what you can call a girl. ______________________

PHONICS Alive at Home Review this Check-Up with your child.

Read Aloud

WHAT IS BROWN?

Brown is the color of
 a country road
Back of a turtle
Back of a toad.
Brown is cinnamon
And morning toast
And the good smell of
The Sunday roast.
Brown is the color of work
And the sound of a river,
Brown is bronze and a bow
And a quiver.
Brown is the house
On the edge of town
Where wind is tearing
The shingles down.

Mary O'Neill

Critical Thinking

How would you color the things outside your home?
What does your favorite color make you think of?

Name ______________________________

Dear Family,

As your child progresses through this unit about colors, she or he will learn about vowel digraphs and diphthongs.

> **vowel digraph:** two letters that come together to make a long sound, a short sound, or a special sound (**bread, hook, pause, lawn**)
>
> **diphthong:** two letters blended together to make one vowel sound (**brown, house, coin, toy**)

- Read the poem "What Is Brown?" on the reverse side. Talk about other colors that you see every day.
- With your child, take turns reading words from the poem that rhyme. **(road/toad, toast/roast, river/quiver, town/down)**
- Help your child find words in the poem that have vowel digraphs or diphthongs. **(brown, good, sound, house, town, down)**

PROJECT

Ask your child to draw a rainbow on a large sheet of paper. When your child learns a word that has a vowel digraph or diphthong, suggest that he or she write it under the rainbow. Your child can practice reading the words and using them in sentences.

Apreciada Familia:

En esta unidad, sobre los colores, su niño aprenderá vocales dígrafas y los diptongos.

> **vocales dígrafas:** dos letras que al unirse producen un sonido largo, corto o especial (**bread, hook, pause, lawn**)
>
> **diptongos:** dos letras que al unirse producen un sonido (**brown, house, coin, toy**)

- Lea la poesía "What Is Brown?" en la página 143. Hablen de los colores que ven todos los días.
- Túrnense para leer palabras que rimen en el poema. **(road/toad, toast/roast, river/quiver, town/down)**
- Ayude al niño a encontrar palabras en el poema con vocales dígrafas y diptongos. **(brown, good, sound, house, town, down)**

PROYECTO

Pida al niño dibujar un arco iris en un papel grande. Cuando el niño aprenda palabras con vocales dígrafas o diptongos puede escribirlas debajo del arco iris. Luego puede practicar leyendo y usando las palabras en oraciones.

Name ______________________________

The vowel digraph **ea** can stand for the short **e** sound, as in **bread**. Listen for the sound of short **e** in the rhyme.

My sister Pam made breakfast—
Bread with green pea spread,
Blue soup with pink potatoes—
I think I'll read instead.

Helpful Hint

A **vowel digraph** is two letters together that stand for one vowel sound. The vowel sound can be long or short, or the vowel digraph can have a sound of its own.

Circle and write the word that names each picture. Color the pictures in which **ea** has the short **e** sound.

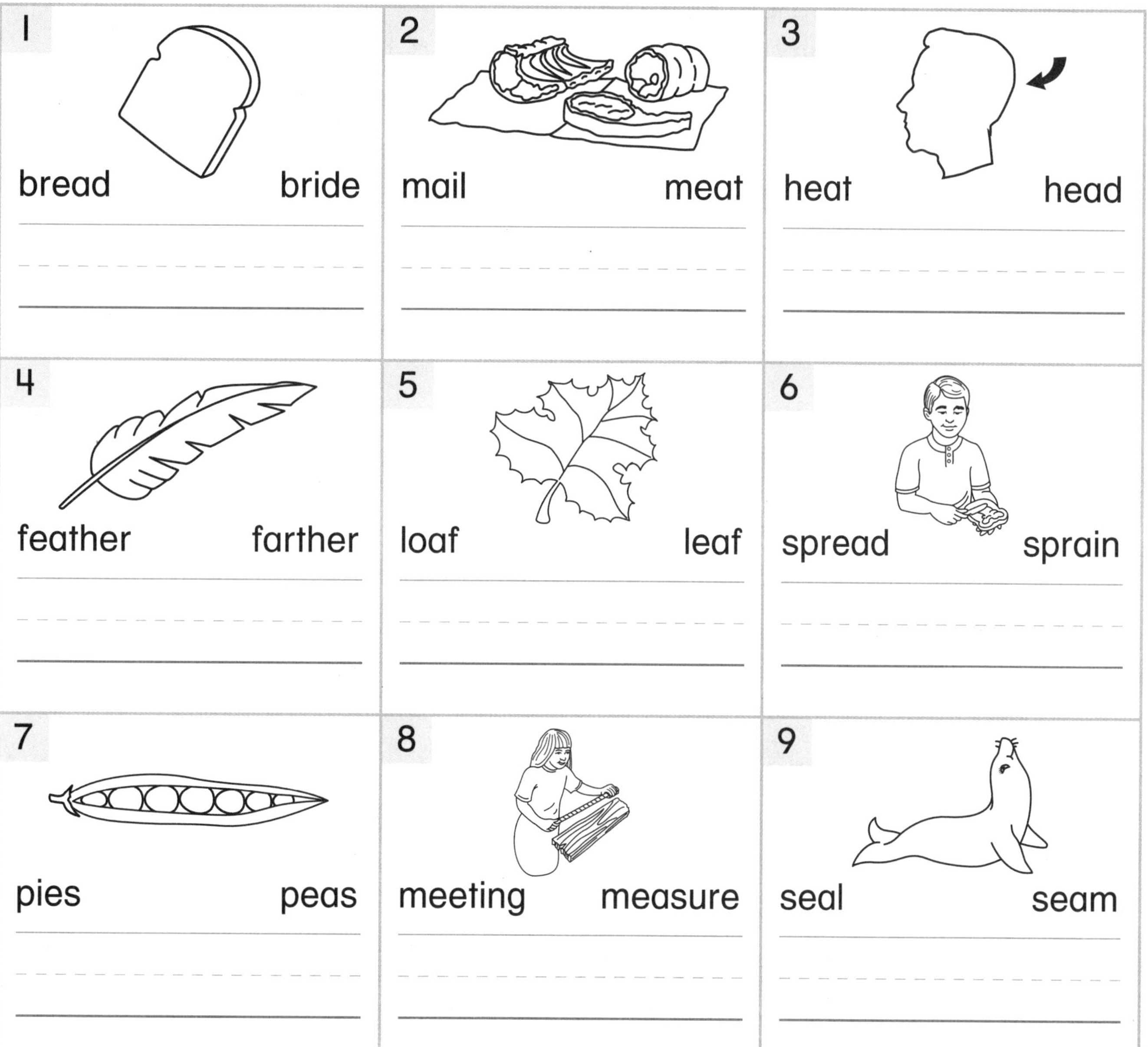

Read the story. Underline the words in which **ea** has the long **e** sound. Write the words in which **ea** has the short **e** sound on the lines below.

Welcome to Rainbow Land

Jean grabbed a leather coat. Joan grabbed a sweater. They went out after breakfast. Something was wrong! The sky was pink instead of blue. The leaves on the trees were silver.

"I'm not ready for this," Jean said. "I'm going back to bed."

"Wait," said Joan. "There's a trail of yellow beans. Let's see where they lead."

Jean and Joan followed the trail to a peach meadow. Just ahead they saw a green gingerbread house.

What happened next? Write about it. Try to use some of these words: **feather, heavy, spread, thread, weather.**

With your child, look in a newspaper or magazine for words with **ea** that have a short **e** sound, such as **head** or **instead.**

Name ______________________________

The vowel digraph **oo** can stand for the vowel sound in **hood** or the vowel sound in **boots.** Listen for the sounds of **oo** in the rhyme.

Janet has a yellow coat,
Which has a purple hood.
Janet has some cool red boots.
Doesn't she look good?

Helpful Hint

A **vowel digraph** is two letters together that stand for one vowel sound. The vowel sound can be long or short, or the vowel digraph can have a sound of its own.

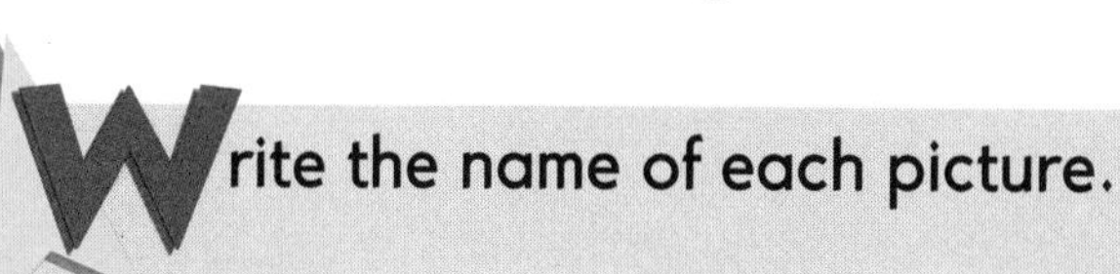

Write the name of each picture.

1 ______	2 ______
3 ______	4 ______
5 ______	6 ______
7 ______	8 ______
9 ______	10 ______
11 ______	12 ______

Write an **oo** word to answer each question. Then take turns with a partner asking and answering the questions.

1. What tool for eating rhymes with **moon**? ______

2. What kind of stream rhymes with **hook**? ______

3. What part of your mouth rhymes with **booth**? ______

4. What place for animals rhymes with **moo**? ______

5. What part of a coat rhymes with **good**? ______

6. What tool for sweeping rhymes with **loom**? ______

Circle and write the word that completes each sentence.

7. A ______ is a kind of seat. spool stool

8. I made a stool from ______. wool wood

9. I sanded it to make it ______. soon smooth

10. I painted it the color of my ______. room root

With your child, make up riddles like the ones at the top of the page for the words **room, wood, book,** and **food.**

Name ______________________________

The vowel digraphs **au** and **aw** can stand for the vowel sound in **Paul** and **dawn**. Listen for the sound of **au** and **aw** in the rhyme.

Bright dawn.
Spotted fawn.
Brown leaves on a lawn.
Paul's autumn day.

Helpful Hint

A **vowel digraph** is two letters together that stand for one vowel sound. The vowel sound can be long or short, or the vowel digraph can have a sound of its own.

Find and write the word that names each picture. In the last box, write the word that is not used and draw a picture to go with it.

August	laundry	claw	lawn	sausage
hawk	saw	launch	straw	

1 ______	2 ______	3 ______
4 ______	5 ______	6 ______
7 AUGUST ______	8 ______	9 ______

Circle the words that have the same vowel sound as **launch** and **straw**.

sauce	clue	haul	play
fault	yawn	head	cause
pause	thread	shawl	breath
jaw	fawn	spread	draw

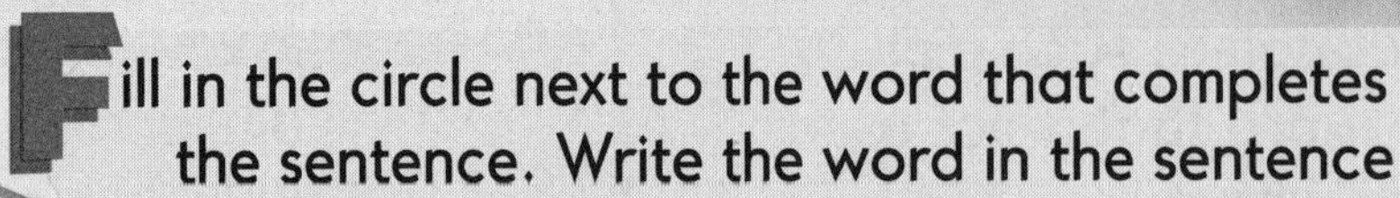

Fill in the circle next to the word that completes the sentence. Write the word in the sentence.

1. Last ________________ I stayed with Aunt Paula. ○ auto ○ autumn

2. We woke up at ________________. ○ drawn ○ dawn

3. We looked out and saw a brown ________________. ○ hawk ○ law

4. It had a hooked beak and sharp ________________. ○ thaws ○ claws

5. We also saw a spotted ________________. ○ fawn ○ yawn

6. It ran across Aunt Paula's ________________. ○ lawn ○ jaw

7. It ________________ to look back at us. ○ caused ○ paused

Write on

Write about something you like to do in the autumn.

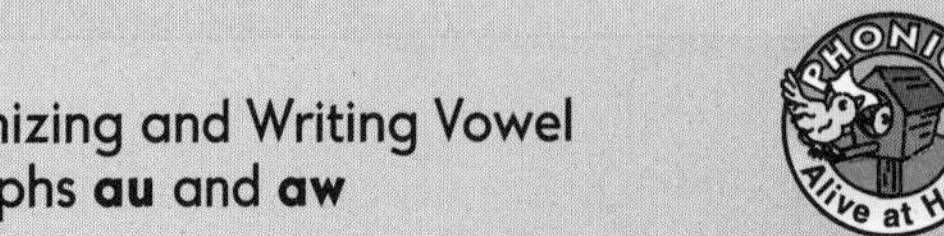

LESSON 80: Recognizing and Writing Vowel Digraphs **au** and **aw**

PHONICS Alive at Home

With your child, make up sentences using the words he or she did not use to fill in the blanks.

Name ______________________________

Write the name of each picture in the puzzle. Then read down to find the answer to the question.

1 ___ ___ ___ ___

2 ___ ___ ___ ___

3 ___ ___ ___ ___

4 ___ ___ ___

5 ___ ___ ___ ___ ___ ___

6 ___ ___ ___ ___ ___ ___

7 ___ ___ ___ ___

8 ___ ___ ___ ___ ___

9 ___ ___ ___ ___ ___ ___ ___

10 ___ ___ ___ ___ ___

What is gray or white and hard to catch?

a ______________ ______________

Color the box that contains the vowel digraph in each picture name. Write the word.

1		2		3	
	ea oo aw		oo au ea		au ea oo
4		**5**		**6**	
	ea oo aw		au oo ea		oo au ea
7		**8**		**9**	
	oo au ea		oo aw ea		au ea oo

Circle the word that fits each clue.

10. You use this to eat.	stood	spoon	soon
11. This is a summer month.	autumn	August	auto
12. You do this on paper.	thaw	straw	draw
13. You can read this.	book	hood	hoof
14. You can put this on.	instead	sweater	thread

PHONICS Alive at Home Review this Check-Up with your child.

Name ____

The diphthong **ow** stands for the vowel sound in **brown**. Listen for the sound of **ow** in the rhyme.

"How now, Brown Cow?" I said,
"Please make my milk pail full."
Oh, how was I to know
That "cow" was a prize bull?

Helpful Hint

A **diphthong** is two letters blended together that stand for one vowel sound.

Say the name of each picture. Circle **Diphthong** if the word has the vowel sound in **brown**. Circle **Long o** if the word has the vowel sound in **snow**.

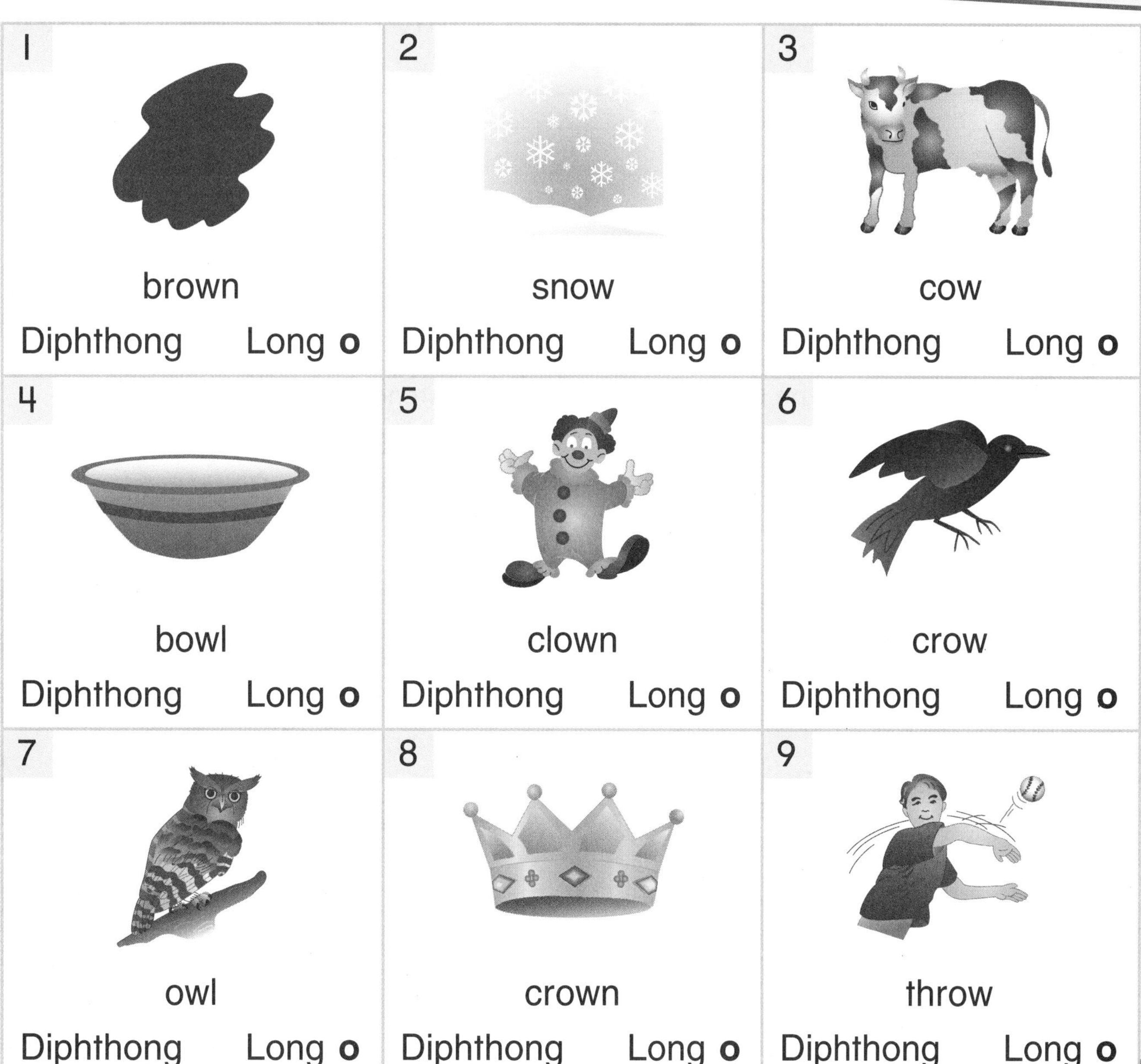

The diphthong **ou** in **couch** stands for the same vowel sound as the diphthong **ow** in **brown**. Listen for the sound of **ou** in the rhyme.

Sleeping on a green couch,
The cat made not a sound,
Until a gray hound found her
And chased her all around.

Helpful Hint

A **diphthong** is two letters blended together that stand for one vowel sound.

Circle the word that names each picture.

1 cloud / claw / clown	2 crane / crown / crowd	3 how / horse / house
4 porch / pouch / peach	5 blouse / blues / blaze	6 cow / cob / couch

Use a word from the box to complete each sentence.

brown	mountains	owl	sound

7. Let's go hiking in the ____________________.

8. Sh! Don't make a ____________________.

9. Maybe we'll hear a ____________________ bear growling.

10. Maybe we'll hear a loud ____________________ hooting.

Write **sound, down, grow, found, flow.** Ask your child which words have the same vowel sound as **cloud.**

Name ___

The diphthongs **oi** and **oy** stand for the vowel sound in **coins** and **toys**. The diphthong **ew** stands for the vowel sound in **new**. Listen for the sounds of **oi, oy,** and **ew** in the rhyme.

Gold coins, gold coins,
Buy some new toys.
Just a few presents
For happy girls and boys.

Helpful Hint

A **diphthong** is two letters blended together that stand for one vowel sound.

Circle and write the word that names each picture.

1 cones coins cans	2 bow boy bee	3 crew stew screw
4 foil foul few	5 toes toys tows	6 boil bowl blew
7 new newt noise	8 print pant point	9 oak oink oil

Make up "colorful" newspaper headlines using words that you circled on this page. For example, "Boy Finds Brown and Red Newt."

Write an **oi, oy,** or **ew** word to answer each question.

1. What kind of silver paper rhymes with **boil**? __________

2. What means "not many" and rhymes with **blew**? __________

3. What can you play with that rhymes with **joy**? __________

4. What means "dirt" and rhymes with **oil**? __________

5. What cat sound rhymes with **chew**? __________

6. What means "male child" and rhymes with **Roy**? __________

Work Together

With a partner, circle and write the word that completes each sentence. Take turns reading your sentences.

7. You can save gold __________. coins joins

8. You can put meat in __________. crew stew

9. You can __________ the circus. enjoy choice

10. You can watch the __________ on TV. flew news

Help your child sort the words he or she wrote into two groups: **oi/oy** words and **ew** words.

Name ______________________________

Look at the picture of the family. Then follow the directions below.

Directions

1. Circle the name of the newspaper.
2. Put an X on the cloud.
3. Color the mountains green.
4. Draw a box around the newt.
5. Color the crown on Mom's blouse yellow.
6. Color the owl brown.
7. Draw some soil in the pot.
8. Draw a hat for the boy.
9. Color the boy's towel blue.
10. Draw a clown on the newspaper.
11. Color the flowers red.
12. Draw a toy in the yard.

Write the name of each picture. Then find and circle the words in the puzzle. Look across and down.

1	2
______	______
3	4
______	______
5	6
______	______
7	8
______	______

b	r	o	w	n	d
o	a	t	o	y	s
y	f	o	i	l	c
c	l	o	u	d	r
c	o	w	b	c	e
h	o	u	s	e	w

PHONICS Alive at Home

Help your child make a word search puzzle with these words: **clown, pouch, coin, joy, blew.**

Name ___________________________________

Use a word from the box to complete each sentence. Then practice reading the sentences aloud.

Before	both	fast	off	sleep	wish

1. ______________ bedtime, I drew a yellow sun in a blue sky.

2. But I cannot ______________ with a bright sun in my room.

3. How ______________ can I draw a night sky instead?

4. I will draw ______________ a moon and a star.

5. I will make a ______________ on the star.

6. Then I will turn ______________ my light and sleep!

Use one or more words from the box to answer the questions.

7. What do you do before you go to sleep at night?

____

8. What do you wish you had in your room?

____

Read and Write

Read the instructions. Then answer the questions.

How to Paint with Straws

First choose a flat work area. Put down newspaper. Then place a piece of shiny shelf paper on top of the newspaper. Now you are ready to paint!

Use a spoon to put a drop of yellow paint on the paper. Next, point the straw at the paint. Then blow gently. The paint will spread out. Pause to let the paint dry. Then repeat with other colors.

When your painting is done, some of the shapes may look like flowers or toys. Use a brown crayon to draw a frame around these shapes.

1. Name one thing you should do before starting to paint.

2. What should you do after your painting is done?

PHONICS Alive at Home

With your child, take turns acting out the steps for making a painting with straws.

Name ________________________________

Say, spell, and talk about each word in the box. Then write each word under the vowels in its name.

about
because
brown
drew
how
join
look
news
saw
spools
thread
toys

1 ea	2 oo	3 au / aw
4 ow / ou	5 oi / oy	6 ew

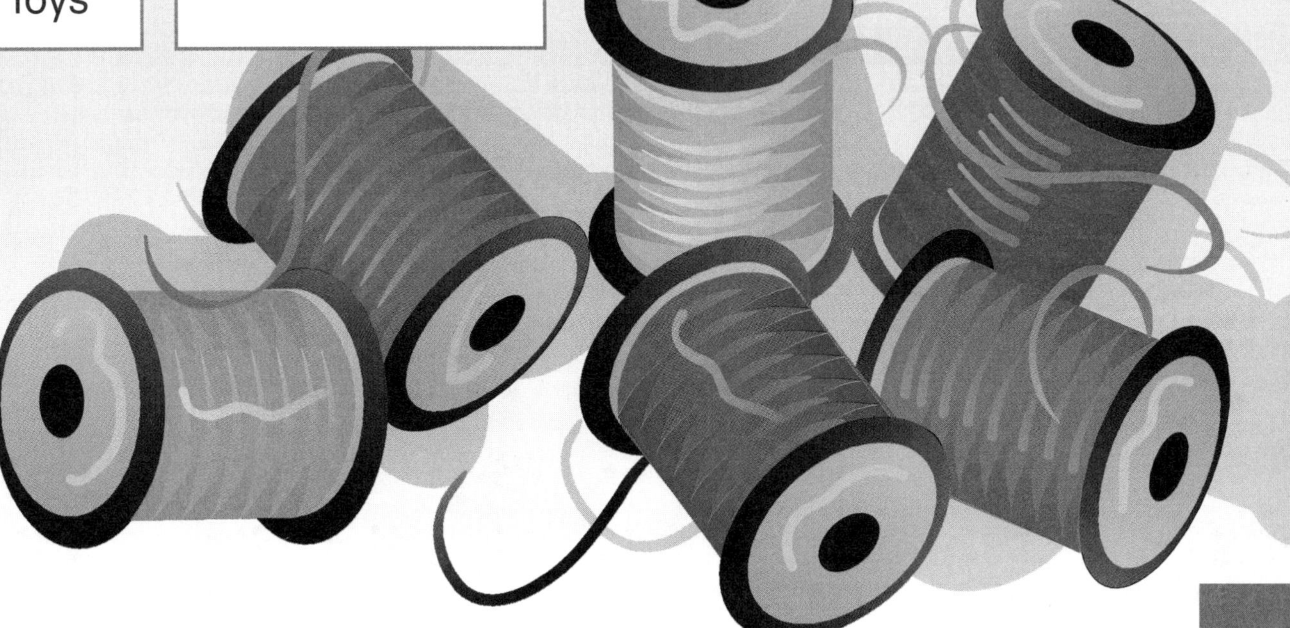

Think of something you can make from spools. Write a paragraph to describe it. Use one or more of your spelling words. Tell a partner what you chose to describe.

about	because	brown	drew	how	join
look	news	saw	spools	thread	toys

I can make

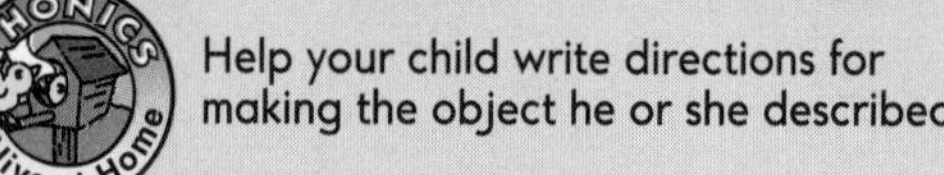

Help your child write directions for making the object he or she described.

Name ______________________________

Look and Learn Let's read and talk about colorful flowers.

Flowers can be many colors. Ground ivy is purple. Snowdrops are white. Some trees have green flowers and leaves. Crown imperials may be red or yellow. Strawflowers may be red, pink, yellow, violet, or white.

Do you enjoy flowers? See if you can plant a garden. Watch it bloom. Look for both birds and butterflies to stop by.

If you had a garden, what would you wish to plant in it? Why?

Circle the words in each list that have the same vowel sound as the picture name.

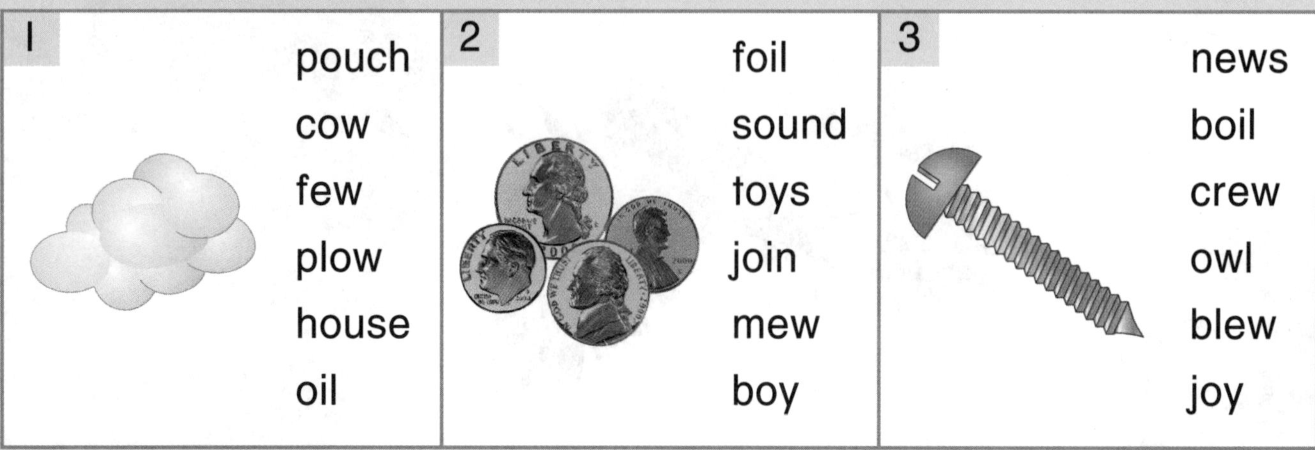

1	2	3
pouch	foil	news
cow	sound	boil
few	toys	crew
plow	join	owl
house	mew	blew
oil	boy	joy

Fill in the circle next to the word that completes the sentence. Write the word in the sentence.

4. Roy ________________ painting pictures. ○ enjoys ○ boils

5. Joy likes looking at ________________. ○ sounds ○ clouds

6. Lew saves shiny new ________________. ○ coins ○ soil

7. Floyd likes ________________ cars. ○ toy ○ noise

8. Joy stays up to see the ________________. ○ news ○ mews

9. Sue enjoys milking the ________________. ○ couch ○ cow

10. Latoya helps make beef ________________. ○ stew ○ flew

PHONICS Alive at Home Review this Check-Up with your child.

Numbers, Numbers

Numbers in the grocery store
　　About the things we eat,
Numbers on the doorways,
　　And in the city street.

Numbers on the calendar,
　　On signs that flash or glow,
Numbers on the telephone,
　　Or tickets for the show.

Numbers on the buses,
　　On money that I spend,
Numbers on the stamps I put
　　On letters that I send.

Numbers on the highways, yes
　　And numbers in a book!
It seems I'm seeing numbers
　　Almost everywhere I look!

Lee Blair

Critical Thinking

Why are numbers important in your life?
What kinds of problems would people have if there were no numbers?

Name ____________________

Dear Family,

As your child progresses through this unit about numbers, he or she will learn about contractions, plurals, and word endings **s**, **ed**, and **ing.**

> **contraction:** two words written as one with one or more letters left out (**isn't = is not; I'll = I will**)
>
> **plural:** word that means more than one (**books, peaches**)
>
> **word endings s, ed, ing:** endings that can be added to a word to make new words (**needs, helped, skipped, jumping, baking**)

- Read the poem "Numbers, Numbers" on the reverse side. Talk about places where you see numbers.
- Read the poem again, with your child chiming in on rhyming lines.
- Together, look for words in the poem that are plurals, such as **numbers** and **buses**. Also find the contraction **I'm** and the word that ends in **ing**, **seeing.**

Apreciada Familia:

En esta unidad, sobre los números, su niño aprenderá sobre contracciones, plurales y palabras que terminan en **s**, **ed**, y **ing.**

> **contracción:** una palabra formada por la abreviación de dos palabras (**isn't = is not; I'll = I will**)
>
> **plural:** palabras que indican más de uno (**books, peaches**)
>
> **palabras que terminan en s, ed, ing:** terminaciones que se añaden al final de una palabra (**needs, helped, skipped, jumping, baking**)

- Lea la poesía "Numbers, Numbers" en la página 165. Hablen de los lugares donde ven números.
- Lean el poema de nuevo, repicando los versos que riman.
- Juntos busquen en el poema palabras en plural como por ejemplo: **numbers** y **buses**. También busquen la contracción **I'm** y la palabra que termina en **ing**, **seeing.**

PROJECT

Make a word bank by putting a slit in the top of a shoebox. When your child learns a new contraction, plural word, or word that ends in **s**, **ed**, or **ing**, have him or her write the word on a card and "deposit" it in the bank. Your child can "withdraw" words and use them in sentences.

PROYECTO

Hagan un banco de palabras con una caja de zapatos. Cada vez que el niño aprenda una contracción, un plural, o una palabra que termine en **s**, **ed**, o **ing**, pídale escribirla en una tarjeta y "depositarla" en el banco. El niño puede "retirar" palabras para escribir oraciones.

Name ______________________________

Didn't is the contraction for **did not.** Listen and look for contractions in the rhyme.

If a 40-foot tree didn't fall,
And you and I weren't near,
How loud would the loudest noise be
That you and I couldn't hear?

A **contraction** is a short way of writing two words as one. In a contraction, one or more letters are left out. An **apostrophe** (') shows where the letters were. Some contractions are formed with **not.**

hasn't = has + not
won't = will + not

Draw a line from each contraction to the pair of words that means the same.

1	didn't	will not	5	isn't	have not
2	hasn't	could not	6	weren't	does not
3	won't	did not	7	haven't	were not
4	couldn't	has not	8	doesn't	is not

Write the contraction for each pair of words.

aren't can't don't shouldn't wasn't wouldn't

9 should not ________	10 was not ________	11 are not ________
12 can not ________	13 would not ________	14 do not ________

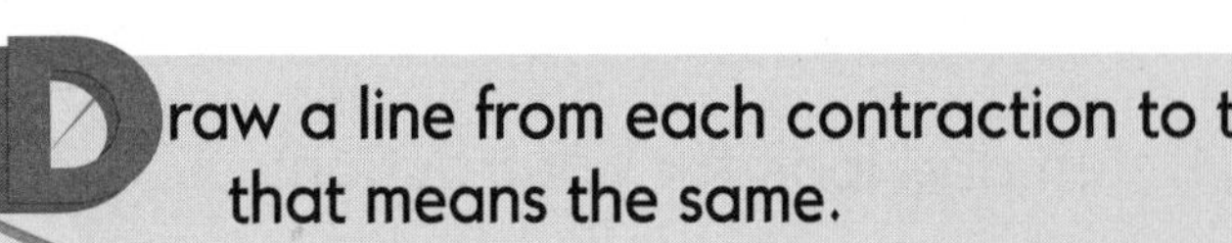

Draw a line from each contraction to the pair of words that means the same.

Helpful Hint

Some contractions are formed with **will.**
she'll = she + will

1	she'll	we will	4	they'll	I will
2	you'll	she will	5	he'll	he will
3	we'll	you will	6	I'll	they will

Write the contraction for the underlined words in each sentence. Then use the bus schedule to write two sentences of your own. Include a contraction in each sentence.

Place	Bus Number
Zoo	57
Downtown	25
Library	12

Place	Bus Number
Pine Lake	15
Museum	32
South Mall	27

7. I will take Bus 12 to the library. ____________

8. She will go downtown on Bus 25. ____________

9. He will take Bus 15 to the lake. ____________

10. Hurry or you will miss the bus! ____________

11. ____

12. ____

PHONICS Alive at Home

Together, use the contractions **I'll, you'll,** and **we'll** to talk about the things you and your child will do tomorrow.

Name ______________________________

With a partner, write the contraction for each pair of words. Take turns reading the pair of words and then the contraction.

Helpful Hint

Some contractions are formed with **am, is,** and **are.**

I'm = I + am
he's = he + is
we're = we + are

he's	they're	I'm	we're	it's	what's	she's	you're	that's

1 I am	2 he is	3 we are
4 that is	5 she is	6 they are
7 it is	8 what is	9 you are

Write the words for the underlined contraction in each sentence.

10. I'm going to run in a race. ______________

11. It's a two-mile run. ______________

12. I hope you're planning to come. ______________

Helpful Hint

Some contractions are formed with **have, has,** and **us.**
she's = she + is or **she + has**
you've = you + have
let's = let + us

Write the contraction for each pair of words.

he's she's it's they've I've we've let's you've

1 she has	2 you have	3 let us
4 we have	5 he has	6 I have
7 they have	8 it has	

Write the words for the underlined contraction in each sentence.

9. I've a new game we can play.

10. You've scored thirty points.

11. It's been fun playing with you.

PHONICS Alive at Home

Make up sentences with **I have, you have,** or **they have.** Ask your child to replace the two words with a contraction.

Name ______________________________

Say, spell, and talk about each word in the box. Then write each word under the correct heading.

can't
didn't
I'll
it's
I've
let's
shouldn't
that's
they've
we've
what's
you'll

1 Contractions with **not**	2 Contractions with **is**	3 Contractions with **have**

4 Contractions with **will**	5 Contraction with **us**

7:30 A.M.

Imagine that your classroom clock could talk. Write what it would say. Use one or more of your spelling words. Then give your speech.

can't	didn't	I'll	it's	I've	let's
shouldn't	that's	they've	we've	what's	you'll

7:30 A.M.

 LESSON 92: Connecting Spelling, Writing, and Speaking

PHONICS Alive at Home

Ask your child questions as if he or she were the classroom clock. Tell your child to answer using spelling words.

Name ______________________

Use the number code to write contractions. Write the letter for each number. Put an apostrophe in the blank space. Then write the words for each contraction.

1 = **a**	2 = **d**	3 = **e**	4 = **h**	5 = **i**
6 = **l**	7 = **n**	8 = **o**	9 = **r**	10 = **s**
11 = **t**	12 = **u**	13 = **v**	14 = **w**	15 = **y**

1. i s n ' t (5 10 7 __ 11) — is — not
2. ___ (14 3 __ 13 3) ______ ______
3. ___ (15 8 12 __ 9 3) ______ ______
4. ___ (10 4 3 __ 6 6) ______ ______
5. ___ (2 5 2 7 __ 11) ______ ______
6. ___ (11 4 3 15 __ 9 3) ______ ______
7. ___ (1 9 3 7 __ 11) ______ ______
8. ___ (6 3 11 __ 10) ______ ______

Draw a line from each contraction to the pair of words that means the same.

1	he'll	she will	9	wasn't	will not
2	she'll	he has	10	you're	was not
3	he's	she has	11	won't	you have
4	she's	he will	12	you've	you are
5	can't	we are	13	I'm	it has
6	couldn't	can not	14	I've	I will
7	we've	could not	15	it's	I am
8	we're	we have	16	I'll	I have

Underline the contraction in each sentence. Then write the words for the contraction.

17. What's your new room number? ____________

18. I don't know mine yet. ____________

19. Tony can't find his room. ____________

20. I'll help him look for it. ____________

21. I think it's down the hall. ____________

PHONICS Alive at Home Review this Check-Up with your child.

Name ______________________________

Stairs is the plural of **stair**. **Porches** is the plural of **porch**. Listen and look for plurals in the rhyme.

On porches stood Lola and Lu.
Each sighed, "I have nothing to do."
So they sat on the stairs
And counted their hairs—4,302!

Helpful Hint

Plural means "more than one." Add **s** to most words to make plurals. Add **es** to words that end in **s, ss, ch, sh, x,** or **z.**

goat + s = goats
peach + es = peaches

Each picture shows more than one. Add **s** or **es** to the word to write the plural for each picture name.

1 goat ______	2 peach ______
3 dish ______	4 shell ______
5 fox ______	6 cone ______
7 fork ______	8 dress ______
9 dime ______	10 bus ______

Change the **y** to **i** and write the plural of each word. Compare answers with a partner.

Helpful Hint

When a word ends in **y** after a consonant, change the **y** to **i** before adding **es.**
penny + es = pennies
baby + es = babies

1 penny	2 baby	3 party
4 story	**5 puppy**	**6 fly**

Add **es** to each word at the left and write the new word in the sentence.

puppy **7.** My dog Fleas had five ____________.

pony **8.** Soon they'll be the size of small ____________.

buddy **9.** The puppies and I are best ____________.

penny **10.** Their fur is the color of shiny ____________!

Write about some baby bunnies. How big are they? What color are they?

Ask your child to explain how to write the plural of these words: **sky, berry, city, cherry.**

Name ______________________________

Write the plural of each picture name in the puzzle. Remember to add **s** or **es** and to make spelling changes. Then read the shaded letters down to find the answer to the question.

1 ___ ___ ___ ___ ___ ___ ___

2 ___ ___ ___ ___ ___ ___

3 ___ ___ ___ ___ ___ ___ ___

4 ___ ___ ___ ___ ___ ___ ___

5 ___ ___ ___ ___ ___

6 ___ ___ ___ ___ ___ ___ ___ ___

7 ___ ___ ___ ___ ___ ___

8 ___ ___ ___ ___ ___

9 ___ ___ ___ ___ ___ ___ ___

10 ___ ___ ___ ___ ___

What number should you call in an emergency?

______ ______ ______

Add **s** or **es** to write the plural of each word. Remember to make spelling changes.

1 pony	2 trunk	3 dress
4 box	5 sack	6 fly
7 bunny	8 peach	9 straw

Add **s** or **es** so that the word in **bold** print makes sense in each sentence.

10. There are 10 **penny** in a dime.

11. Some **fly** live only about 2 hours.

12. **Fox** live about 7 years.

13. Newborn **baby** have 300 bones.

14. There are more than 12,000 kinds of **ant**.

PHONICS Alive at Home Review this Check-Up with your child.

Name ______________________________

Bats has the ending **s. Pitches** has the ending **es.** Listen and look for words with the endings **s** and **es** in the rhyme.

Tom pitches. Pam bats.
She hits a big home run.
And as she slides into home plate,
Her team wins two to one!

Helpful Hint

A base word is a word to which endings like **s** and **es** may be added to make new words.

help + s = helps
fix + es = fixes

Add **s** or **es** to each base word. Write the new word.

1 help ______	2 fix ______
3 brush ______	4 buzz ______
5 find ______	6 mix ______

Underline the word ending in **s** or **es** in each sentence. Write the base word.

7. Nikki hits the ball with a crack. ______

8. She quickly drops the bat. ______

9. She reaches first base safely. ______

Learning has the ending **ing.** Listen and look for words with the ending **ing** in the rhyme.

Jim was learning how to count.
Jen taught him what to do.
Thanking her, Jim said to Jen,
"I'm counting now on you!"

Helpful Hint

The ending **ing** can be added to a base word.
help + ing = helping

Add **ing** to each base word. Write the new word.

1 help ________	2 fix ________
3 jump ________	4 grow ________
5 find ________	6 pass ________

Underline the word ending in **ing** in each sentence. Write the base word.

7. June is helping Azeem do math. ________

8. They are adding numbers. ________

9. June and Azeem are trying to solve a problem. ________

10. They like working together. ________

PHONICS Alive at Home

Say the following words: **reading, sleeping, fishing.** Have your child act out each word and then write it.

Name ______________________________

Kicked has the ending **ed.** Listen and look for words with the ending **ed** in the rhyme.

Victor kicked the soccer ball.
His team won nine to eight.
Victor's fans jumped up and cheered,
"We think that Victor's great!"

Helpful Hint

The ending **ed** can be added to a base word to tell about the past.
sail + ed = sailed

Tell what Lauren and Keisha did in the past. Add **ed** to each base word. Write the new word below.

Things Lauren Did at the Lake	Things Keisha Did in the Kitchen
sail splash float	wash mix cook
1 ______	4 ______
2 ______	5 ______
3 ______	6 ______

Add **ed** to each base word and write the new word in the sentence.

push **7.** Jon ______________ the buttons on the phone.

reach **8.** He ______________ his friend Abdul's home.

ask **9.** He ______________ to speak to Abdul.

Change the **y** to **i** and add **es** and **ed** to each base word. Write the new word. Compare answers with a partner.

Helpful Hint

When a base word ends in **y** after a consonant, change the **y** to **i** before adding **es** or **ed.**

dry + es = dries
dry + ed = dried

	es	ed
1 dry		
2 carry		
3 fry		
4 marry		

Underline the word ending in **es** or **ed** in each sentence. Write the base word.

5. Yesterday Stacy copied a math puzzle. ______

6. Then she hurried home from school. ______

7. Today she tries to solve the puzzle. ______

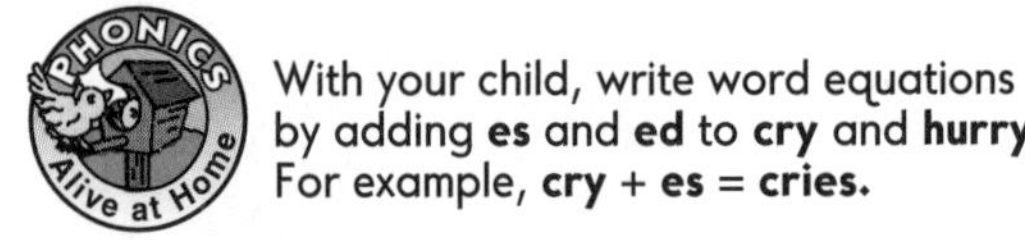

With your child, write word equations by adding **es** and **ed** to **cry** and **hurry**. For example, **cry** + **es** = **cries**.

Name ______________________________

When a base word ends in **e**, drop the final **e** before adding **ing** or **ed**.
save + ing = saving
save + ed = saved

Drop the final **e** and add **ing** and **ed** to each base word. Write the new word.

	ing	ed
1 save	______	______
2 hike	______	______
3 use	______	______
4 chase	______	______

Use a word from above to complete each sentence. Then read the story.

I am going ______________ today with Jill. Last time we ______________, I saw three squirrels. I ______________ a camera to take their picture.

Write about things you might see on a hiking trip. Complete this sentence: "If I go hiking, I might see . . . ."

Double the final consonant and add **ing** and **ed** to each base word. Write the new word. Then compare answers with a partner

Helpful Hint

If a short vowel word ends in a single consonant, usually double the final consonant before adding **ing** or **ed.**

hop + ing = hopping
hop + ed = hopped

	ing	ed
1 hop		
2 wag		
3 grab		
4 stop		

Underline the word ending in **ing** or **ed** in each sentence. Write the base word.

5. Yesterday I jogged in the park. ____________

6. Today I will go swimming. ____________

7. I am getting a lot of exercise! ____________

Ask your child to **hum, tap,** and **skip.** Then help him or her write the words with the endings **ing** and **ed.**

Name ________________________________

Say each word. Write the number of syllables you hear. Then answer the question below.

	s or es		ing		ed	
1	walks	☐	walking	☐	walked	☐
2	tries	☐	trying	☐	tried	☐
3	races	☐	racing	☐	raced	☐
4	votes	☐	voting	☐	voted	☐
5	shops	☐	shopping	☐	shopped	☐

6. How many syllables are in words with endings? Circle the best answer.

always one   always two   one or more

Add **ed** or **ing** to each base word and write the new word in the sentence.

bake **7.** We are ________________ muffins today.

mix **8.** I ________________ two cups of flour and water.

place **9.** Dad just ________________ the pan in the oven.

Complete each column by adding the ending at the top to the base word.

	s or **es**	**ing**	**ed**
1 paint			
2 rush			
3 chase			
4 try			

Write the base word.

5 sleeps	6 winning	7 flipped
8 making	9 pitches	10 saved
11 quitting	12 dries	13 studied

PHONICS Alive at Home

Ask your child to group the words in items 5–13 under the headings **s/es, ing, ed.**

Name ____________________

Use a word from the box to complete each sentence. Then practice reading the sentences aloud.

call	many	read	those	upon	write

1. How ____________ pennies can I save today?

2. How many times can I ____________ out, "Let's play"?

3. How many stories can I ____________ with my pen?

4. How many books can I ____________ before I'm ten?

5. How many stars can I wish ____________ tonight?

6. Can I count ____________ stars shining so bright?

Use one or more words from the box to answer the questions.

7. How many books can you read this week?

____

8. How many stories can you write this week?

____

Read the number log that Mark kept for math class.
Then answer the questions.

Numbers All Around

At Home

- I used the numbers on my watch to get to school on time. I started walking at 7:15.
- I invited grandma for dinner by dialing her phone number. She'll be coming at 7:00 tonight.
- I didn't forget Gary's birthday. I looked at the calendar. It's tomorrow— March 29th! He'll be nine.

At School

- I got to my classroom by finding a 4 on the door.
- I found my math lesson by turning to page 133.
- I kept score during soccer by counting the goals.

Foxes: 3 Ponies: 6

1. Name one way Mark used numbers at home.

2. How do numbers help you at home?

PHONICS Alive at Home

With your child, keep a number log.
Think of ways to group your findings.

Name ______________________________

Say, spell, and talk about each word in the box. Then write each word under the correct heading.

brushes
carried
hurried
jogging
jumping
raked
running
smiling
stopped
tries
washed
wiped

1 No Base Changes	2 Change **y** to **i**

3 Drop Final **e**	4 Double Final Consonant

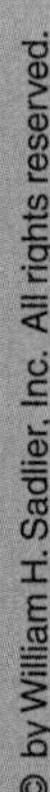

Read the playground rhyme. Then add one or two verses. Use one or more of your spelling words. Share your rhyme with the class.

brushes	carried	hurried	jogging	jumping	raked
running	smiling	stopped	tries	washed	wiped

I went outside to count the stars.
I made a mistake and counted cars.
I went inside to bake a pie.
I made a mistake and baked a fly.

Ask your child to read the rhyme he or she wrote. Together, make up a new verse using some of the spelling words.

Name ____________________

Look and Learn

Let's read and talk about clocks.

What time is it? Let's read a clock to find out. Analog clocks have faces with numbers 1 to 12 and hands that point to the minutes and the hour. Digital clocks don't have hands. A : separates the hour and minutes. The number before the : tells the hour. The number after the : tells the minutes past the hour.

What would happen if people didn't have clocks or watches?

Check-Up Add the ending at the top to each base word in the column.

s or **es**	**ing**	**ed**
1 clean	4 bake	7 stop
2 mix	5 know	8 jump
3 cry	6 drip	9 wipe

Underline the word ending in **ing** or **ed** in each sentence. Then write the base word.

10. At 7:00 A.M., Tina's alarm clock buzzed.

11. She reached for the clock on the table.

12. She used both hands, but she couldn't find it.

13. Where was the clock hiding?

14. Tina tried to go back to sleep.

PHONICS Alive at Home Review this Check-Up with your child.

Read Aloud

from
Swinging

Slowly, slowly, swinging low,
Let me see how far I go!
Slowly, slowly, keeping low,
I see where the wild flowers grow!

(Getting quicker):
Quicker, quicker,
Swinging higher,
I can see
The sunset's fire!

Faster, faster,
Through the air,
I see almost
Everywhere.

(Getting slower):
Slower, slower, now I go,
Swinging, dreaming, getting low;
Slowly, slowly, down I go–
Till I touch the grass below.

Irene Thompson

Critical Thinking

What do you think is the best part about going high on a swing?
If you could put a swing anywhere, where would you put it? Why?

Name ______________________________

Dear Family,

As your child progresses through this unit about outdoor fun, she or he will learn about the following:

suffix: word part added to the end of a word to change its meaning or make a new word (**careful**)

prefix: word part added to the beginning of a word to change its meaning or make a new word (**reload**)

synonyms: words that have the same meaning (**fast/quick**)

antonyms: words that have the opposite meaning (**up/down**)

homonyms: words that sound the same but have different spellings and meanings (**blue/blew**)

- Read the poem "Swinging" on the reverse side. Talk about how your family has outdoor fun.
- Read the poem again, going faster and faster until you reach the last stanza.
- Together, look for words in the poem with the suffixes **ly** and **er**, such as slowly and quicker.

Apreciada Familia:

En esta unidad, sobre el recreo, su niño aprenderá los siguientes otros tipos de palabras y partes de palabras.

sufijos: letras que se añaden al final de una palabra y que cambian su significado o hacen una nueva (**careful**)

prefijos: letras que se añaden al principio de una palabra y que cambian su significado o hacen una nueva (**reload**)

sinónimos: palabras que tienen el mismo significado (**fast/quick**)

antónimos: palabras que significan lo opuesto (**up/down**)

homónimos: palabras que tienen el mismo sonido pero diferente significado y se escriben diferentes (**blue/blew**)

- Lea "Swinging" en la página 193. Hablen de lo que hace su familia para divertirse fuera de la casa.
- Lea de nuevo el poema, cada vez más rápido, hasta que llegue a la última estrofa.
- Busquen palabras en el poema que tengan los sufijos **ly**, **er**, por ejemplo: slowly, quicker.

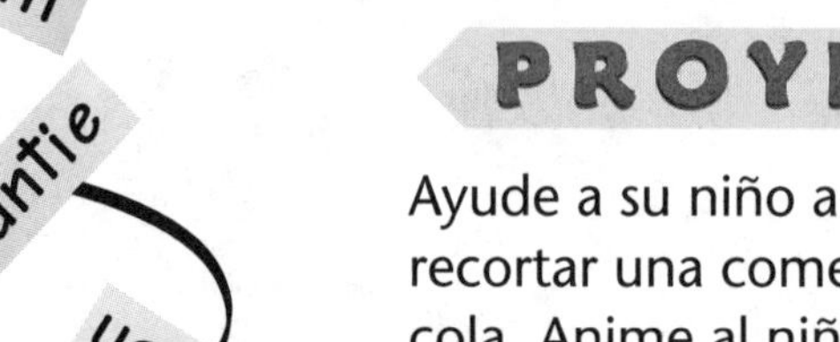

PROJECT

Help your child draw a kite and cut it out. Attach a tail. As your child learns new words from this unit, have him or her write the words on small pieces of paper and tape them to the tail.

PROYECTO

Ayude a su niño a dibujar y recortar una cometa. Atele una cola. Anime al niño a escribir palabras aprendidas en esta unidad en pedacitos de papel y pegarlas en la cola de la cometa.

Name ___________________________________

Cheerful ends with the suffix **ful.** Listen and look for the suffixes **ful, less, ness,** and **ly** in the rhyme.

My puppy is so cheerful,
His gladness always shows.
We play for endless hours,
Then off he quickly goes.

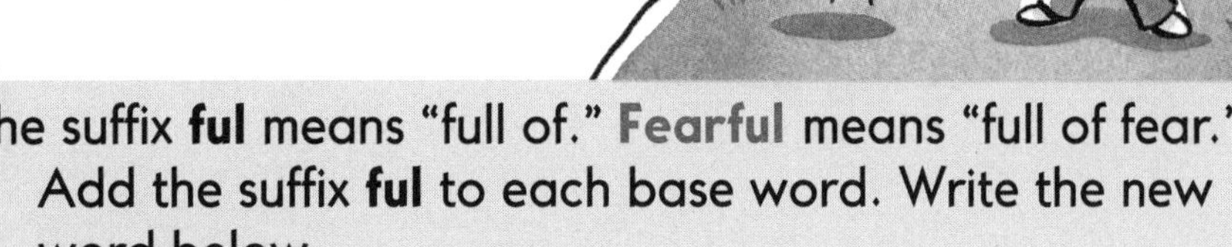

The suffix **ful** means "full of." **Fearful** means "full of fear." Add the suffix **ful** to each base word. Write the new word below.

Helpful Hint

A **suffix** is a word part added to the **end** of a base word to change its meaning or make a new word.

fear + ful = fearful

Words that Describe People or Things	Words that Describe Feelings
grace help play use	cheer fear hope thank
1 ______	5 ______
2 ______	6 ______
3 ______	7 ______
4 ______	8 ______

Write about the puppy. Use a word that ends in the suffix **ful.**

The suffix **less** means "without." **Fearless** means "without fear." The suffix **ness** means "a state of being." **Softness** means "being soft." Find and write the word that goes with each definition.

Helpful Hint

The suffixes **less** and **ness** can be added to the end of a base word.

fear + less = fearless
soft + ness = softness

cloudless	darkness	fearless	loudness	softness	useless

1 without fear	2 being soft	3 being loud
4 without use	5 without clouds	6 being dark

Work Together

Use a word from above to complete each sentence. Read each word you wrote and have a partner say the base word.

7. Cleo is a brave and ______________ hunter.

8. Don't be fooled by the ______________ of her fur.

9. It's ______________ to try to keep her indoors.

10. She goes out and hunts on sunny, ______________ days.

11. She goes out and hunts in the ______________ of the night.

PHONICS Alive at Home

Ask your child to add **less** to the end of **sleep, noise,** and **seed.** Discuss how **less** changes each word's meaning.

Name ______________________________

The suffix **ly** means "in a certain way." **Softly** means "in a soft way." Add the suffix **ly** to a base word from the box and write a new word to answer the question.

Helpful Hint

The suffix **ly** can be added to the end of a base word.
soft + ly = softly

bright	glad	loud	soft

1. How does snow fall? ______________
2. How does the sun shine? ______________
3. How does thunder boom? ______________
4. How do you greet a friend? ______________

brave	quick	slow	sweet

5. How does a snail crawl? ______________
6. How does a hero act? ______________
7. How does a deer run? ______________
8. How does a bird sing? ______________

Write on

Write a question of your own that can be answered with a word that ends in **ly**. Exchange questions with a classmate.

Faster ends with the suffix **er**. **Fastest** ends with suffix **est**. Listen and look for the suffixes **er** and **est** in the rhyme.

Faster than the fastest train,
Swifter than a jet,
Larry running from a bee
Is the quickest yet!

Helpful Hint

The suffix **er** is added to a base word to compare two things. The suffix **est** is added to compare more than two things.

small smaller smallest

Compare the things. Add **er** or **est** to the base word and write the new word.

1	2	3
small		

Add **er** and **est** to each base word. Write the new word.

	er	est
4. fast		
5. cold		
6. soft		
7. kind		

With your child, make up a story about a race among three animals. Use the words **slow, slower,** and **slowest.**

Name ________________________________

Helpful Hint

Sometimes you need to make spelling changes before adding **er** and **est.**

wet + er = wetter
wet + est = wettest
sunny + er = sunnier
sunny + est = sunniest

Work Together

Double the final consonant and add **er** and **est** to each word. Write the new words. Then compare answers with a partner.

	er	est
1. wet		
2. thin		
3. big		
4. hot		

Change the **y** to **i** and add **er** and **est** to each word. Write the new words.

	er	est
5. sunny		
6. lucky		
7. happy		

Write On

Draw three pictures to show the meaning of **wet, wetter, wettest.** Write sentences to go with your pictures.

Add the suffix to the base word to write a new word. Then say the word. Write the number of syllables you hear.

1	harm + ful	4	neat + ly
2	seed + less	5	high + er
3	sick + ness	6	tall + est

Circle the suffix in each word. Then answer the question below.

7	careful	11	darker	15	kindness
8	wisely	12	joyful	16	sooner
9	homeless	13	shortest	17	safely
10	brightness	14	careless	18	deepest

19. How many syllables does each suffix that you circled add to the base word? Circle the best answer.

none   one   two

Write the words above on paper strips. Ask your child to cut apart the strips to divide the words into syllables.

Name ______________________________

Find and write the word that goes with each definition.

bravely	cheerful	fearless	hopeful	kindness
loudness	sadly	slowly	useless	

1 without fear	2 being loud	3 in a slow way
4 full of cheer	5 in a sad way	6 without use
7 being kind	8 full of hope	9 in a brave way

Add **er** and **est** to each base word. Write the new word. Remember to make spelling changes if you need to.

	er	**est**
10. cold		
11. hot		
12. messy		

Check-Up Write the base word for each word.

1 fearful	2 slowly	3 useless
4 darkness	5 cloudless	6 cheerful
7 bravely	8 fearless	9 loudness
10 hopeful	11 quickly	12 softness

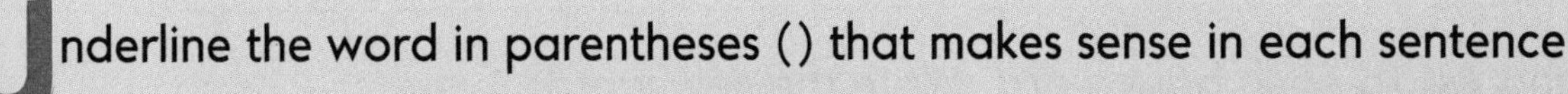

Underline the word in parentheses ( ) that makes sense in each sentence.

13. It was the (**hottest, hotter**) day of the year.

14. I (**gladly, neatly**) agreed to go for a ride with my Uncle Al.

15. We went up (**highest, high**) in the sky in a hot-air balloon.

16. We flew (**faster, fast**) than the wind.

17. I think I'm the (**luckiest, luckier**) person in the world.

18. I won't forget my uncle's (**kindness, loudness**).

Review this Check-Up with your child.

Name ______________________________

Rebuild begins with the prefix **re.** Listen and look for the prefixes **re, un,** and **dis** in the rhyme.

Let's dry off the tent
And rebuild it together.
I'm not unhappy camping.
I just dislike the weather.

Helpful Hint

A **prefix** is a word part added to the **beginning** of a base word to change its meaning or make a new word.

re + tie = retie

The prefix **re** means "again." **Retie** means "tie again." Use the prefix **re** to write a word for each definition.

1 tie again	2 tell again	3 join again
______	______	______
4 place again	**5 load again**	**6 use again**
______	______	______

Add the prefix **re** to each base word and write the new word in the sentence.

pack **7.** Josh had to ______________ his backpack.

fill **8.** Deb had to ______________ the canteens.

tie **9.** We'll leave as soon as I ______________ my shoe.

The prefix **un** means "not" or "to do the opposite of." **Unhappy** means "not happy." **Unpack** is the opposite of **pack.** Add the prefix **un** to the word in **bold** print to complete each sentence.

Helpful Hint

The prefix **un** can be added to the beginning of a base word.

un + happy = unhappy

1. Someone who is not **happy** is ________________.

2. The opposite of **pack** is ________________.

3. If something is not **safe,** it's ________________.

4. The opposite of **roll** is ________________.

5. If you are not **able** to swim, you are ________________ to swim.

Work Together

Add the prefix **un** to each base word and write the new word in the sentence. Take turns with a partner reading the complete sentences.

safe **6.** Without a helmet, skating is ________________.

able **7.** I've looked, but I'm ________________ to find my helmet.

pack **8.** I guess I'll ________________ my skating gear.

roll **9.** I'll ________________ my sleeping bag and camp out instead.

Phonics Alive at Home

Read a word that your child wrote and ask him or her to explain its meaning.

Name ______________________________

Helpful Hint

The prefix **dis** can be added to the beginning of a base word.
dis + **honest** = **dishonest**

The prefix **dis** means "not" or "do the opposite of." **Dishonest** means "not honest." **Disagree** is the opposite of **agree**. Use the prefix **dis** to write a word for each definition.

1 not honest	2 the opposite of **agree**	3 the opposite of **obey**
4 the opposite of **like**	5 not pleased	6 the opposite of **appear**

Add the prefix **dis** so that the word in **bold** print makes sense in each sentence. Write the new word.

7. Ed and I are friends even when we **agree**. ______________

8. I get upset when my dog **obeys** me. ______________

9. It is **honest** to tell a lie. ______________

10. Snow **appears** when it gets warm. ______________

Write one thing you **like** and one thing you **dislike** about the outdoors.

Add the prefix to the base word to write a new word. Then say the word. Write the number of syllables you hear.

1 re + read	4 dis + trust
2 dis + like	5 un + lucky
3 un + fair	6 re + open

Circle the prefix in each word. Then answer the question below.

7 unchain	11 rebuild	15 retell
8 reheat	12 dishonest	16 uncover
9 displeased	13 unfold	17 disapprove
10 rewrite	14 disagree	18 unclear

19. How many syllables does each prefix that you circled add to the base word? Circle the best answer.

none   one   two

Say the words in items 7–18 and ask your child to tell how many syllables he or she hears in each word.

Name ____________________

Write a word with the prefix **re, un,** or **dis** for each clue. Then read down to find the answer to the question.

1 join again ___ ___ ___ ___ ___ ___

2 opposite of **tie** ___ ___ ___ ___ ___

3 opposite of **trust** ___ ___ ___ ___ ___ ___ ___ ___

4 draw again ___ ___ ___ ___ ___ ___

5 opposite of **load** ___ ___ ___ ___ ___ ___

6 opposite of **obey** ___ ___ ___ ___ ___ ___ ___

7 not true ___ ___ ___ ___ ___ ___

8 fill again ___ ___ ___ ___ ___ ___

9 use again ___ ___ ___ ___ ___

10 not able ___ ___ ___ ___ ___ ___

What can you do in the summer sun?

Have a lot of ____________ ____________!

Check-Up Write the base word for each word.

1 retell	2 unpack	3 disobey
4 untie	5 disagree	6 recheck
7 dishonest	8 refill	9 unbutton

Underline the word in parentheses () that makes sense in each sentence.

10. Mom says that my treehouse is (**unable, unsafe**).

11. That (**disagrees, displeases**) Mom.

12. It makes me (**unhappy, unroll**), too.

13. We have to (**reuse, replace**) wood that has rotted.

14. We have to (**repaint, replay**) the whole thing.

15. I (**dislike, disappear**) this sandpaper.

16. I'm (**untied, unable**) to reach the roof.

17. It's (**unclear, unafraid**) how we'll ever finish.

18. I'd better stop complaining and (**refill, rejoin**) Mom at work.

Review this Check-Up with your child.

Name ______________________________

Bag and **sack** are synonyms. Listen and look for synonyms in the rhyme.

Let's run quickly,
In a bag or a sack.
We'll go very fast,
On a path or a track.

Helpful Hint

Synonyms are words that have the same or nearly the same meaning.

Fast and **quick** are synonyms. Find and write a synonym for each word.

bag	begin	fast	home	jog	large

1 quick ______	2 run ______	3 start ______
4 big ______	5 sack ______	6 house ______

Draw a line from each word in the first column to its synonym in the second column.

7	jump	happy	13	cry	weep
8	rush	leap	14	sound	high
9	glad	hurry	15	tall	noise
10	boat	kind	16	wet	yell
11	nice	close	17	sick	ill
12	near	ship	18	shout	damp

Circle the word in each list that means the same or nearly the same as the word in **bold** print.

1 **home**	2 **below**	3 **leave**	4 **pail**
door	over	stay	bucket
house	in	here	spoon
car	under	go	water
work	out	slow	sink

Write the word from the box that is a synonym for the word in **bold** print.

hike	little	pal	tapped	trail

5. My **friend** Goldie likes to be outdoors. ____________

6. One day Goldie went for a **walk.** ____________

7. She decided to explore a new **path.** ____________

8. She followed the path to a **small** house. ____________

9. Goldie **knocked** on the door. ____________

Was anyone home? Finish the story. In your sentences, you might use synonyms for the words **big** and **small.**

Ask your child to read sentences 5–9 using the synonyms he or she wrote in place of the words in bold print.

Name ______________________________

High and **low** are antonyms. Listen and look for antonyms in the rhyme.

High, low, fast, slow,
Over the ocean,
Under the sea,
Hurry up. Come jump with me.

Helpful Hint

Antonyms are words that have the opposite or nearly the opposite meaning.

Hot and **cold** are antonyms. Find and write an antonym for each word.

asleep open big smile float stop hot under left

1 cold	2 awake	3 right
4 go	5 little	6 over
7 frown	8 sink	9 close

Circle the word in each list that means the opposite of the word in **bold** print.

10 **happy**	11 **clean**	12 **lost**	13 **front**
good	water	gone	back
glad	wash	found	door
sad	dirty	under	top

Read about Cam. Then work with a partner to write a story about her friend Mac. Tell how he is the opposite of Cam. Replace each word in bold print with an antonym.

Cam is a **tall girl. She** sits in the **last** row of **her** class. **She** has **long** hair and freckles. **She always** wears glasses. When **she** writes, **she** uses **her right** hand.

Cam likes **winter** sports. **She** enjoys skating. Even on the **coldest** days, you'll find Cam outdoors.

Mac is a short boy.

PHONICS Alive at Home

Ask your child to read each word in bold print and then the antonym he or she wrote. For example: **tall/short, girl/boy.**

Name ______________________________

Heard and **herd** are homonyms. Listen and look for homonyms in the rhyme.

I heard a herd of skunks.
I heard them, I insist!
Though mist hid them from view,
My nose knows what I missed.

Helpful Hint

Homonyms are words that sound the same but have different spellings and meanings.

Sail and **sale** are homonyms. Find and write a homonym for each word.

ate	for	not	sail	sun	to

1 sale	2 eight	3 knot
______	______	______
4 four	**5** son	**6** two
______	______	______

Cross out the word that does not make sense in each sentence. Find and write a homonym from above.

7. I eight breakfast early in the morning. ______

8. Then I decided to go four a walk. ______

9. The son was shining brightly. ______

10. It was a great day two be outdoors. ______

Circle two words in each box that sound the same but have different spellings and meanings.

1			2			3		
	tale	tall		ride	right		reed	road
	tail	tell		write	white		ride	rode
4	knot	note	5	dear	deep	6	weed	weak
	night	knight		deer	deal		week	wood

Circle and write the word that completes each sentence. Compare answers with a partner.

7. Lashanda and I ______________ little toy boats. made maid

8. Mine was red and hers was ______________. blew blue

9. We put paper ______________ on the top. sales sails

10. We put our boats in the ______________. creek creak

11. We decided to race ______________ boats. hour our

12. The wind ______________ the sails. blew blue

13. Lashanda and ______________ clapped. eye I

14. Lashanda ______________ the race. one won

PHONICS Alive at Home

With your child, make up sentences using the words he or she did not circle in items 7–14.

Name ______________________________

Write a word from the box for each clue in the puzzles.

cry	fast	first	hot	lost	plain
rode	sale	sea	stop	under	wet

ACROSS

1. Opposite of **go**
4. Opposite of **slow**
5. Means **below**

DOWN

1. Sounds like **see**
2. Sounds like **plane**
3. Means **damp**

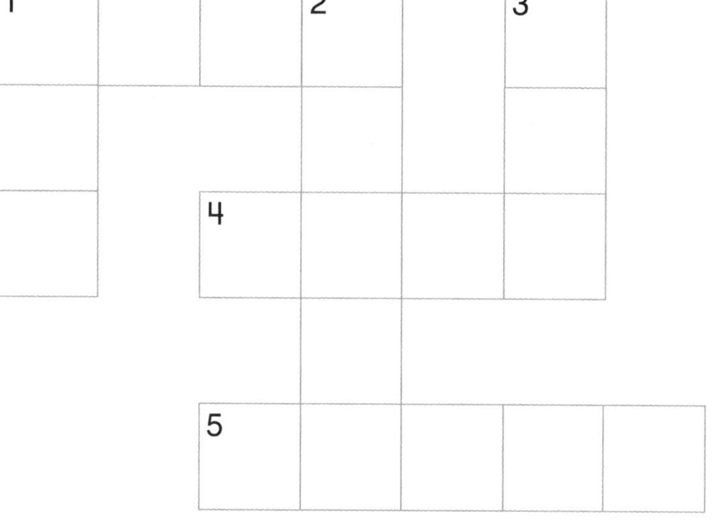

ACROSS

6. Opposite of **last**
10. Opposite of **found**
11. Sounds like **road**

DOWN

7. Sounds like **sail**
8. Opposite of **cold**
9. Means **weep**

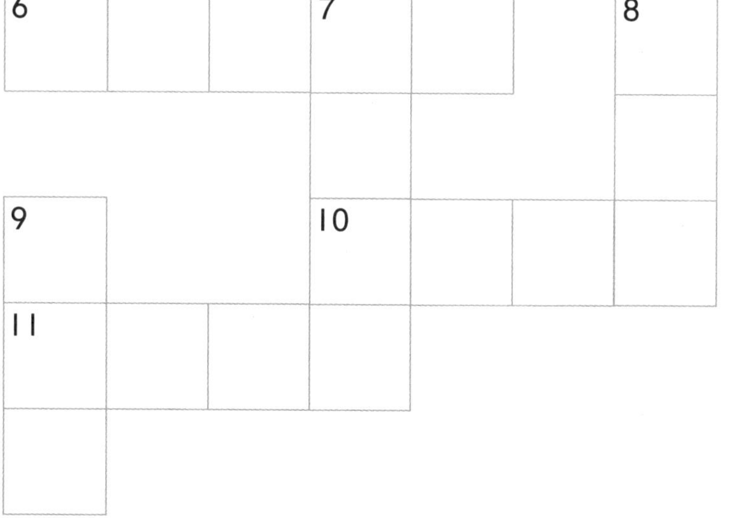

Write a sentence using two or more homonyms. For example, "We **rode** down the **road** and saw a **plane** land on the **plain.**"

Draw a line from a word in the first column to its **synonym** in the second column.

1	home	nap	4	bag	begin
2	sleep	ill	5	friend	pal
3	sick	house	6	start	sack

Draw a line from a word in the first column to its **antonym** in the second column.

7	little	front	10	out	open
8	long	big	11	close	in
9	back	short	12	awake	asleep

Cross out the word that does not make sense in each sentence. Find and write the correct word.

I	made	new	to	wood

13. Dad maid a swing for me. ______

14. He used a piece of would for the seat. ______

15. Dad and eye hung the swing in a tree. ______

16. I like my knew swing. ______

17. Watch me swing two and fro. ______

PHONICS Alive at Home: Ask your child to name a synonym and an antonym for each of these words: **cold, big, fast, start.**

Name ______________________________

Use a word from the box to complete each sentence. Then practice reading the sentences aloud.

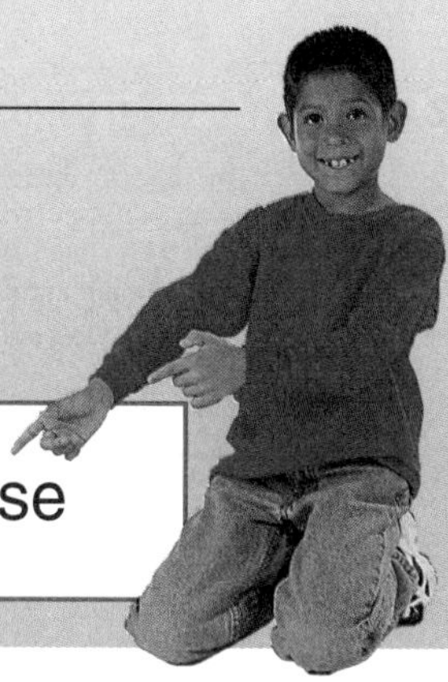

been	cold	five	goes	pull	these

1. It is snowy and ______________ in the park.

2. I've ______________ making the biggest snowman.

3. I made the arms with ______________ sticks.

4. I made a mouth with these ______________ stones.

5. My scarf ______________ around the neck.

6. Don't ______________ it off, or I'll need to retie it!

Use one or more words from the box to answer the questions.

7. What do you like to do on a cold day?

____

8. Where does your family go for outdoor fun?

____

Read and Write Read the book report. Then answer the questions.

Book Report by Leah Siegel

Owl Moon by Jane Yolen

Whoo! Whoo! Did you ever hear the sound of an owl? In Owl Moon by Jane Yolen, a girl and her father go owling. That means they go looking for owls. It is a snowy night and the woods look scary. But the girl is not afraid. She and her father keep walking and looking.

You will like this book if you like to read about animals or about doing things outdoors. Read Owl Moon to find out if the girl ever sees an owl. Whoo! Whoo!

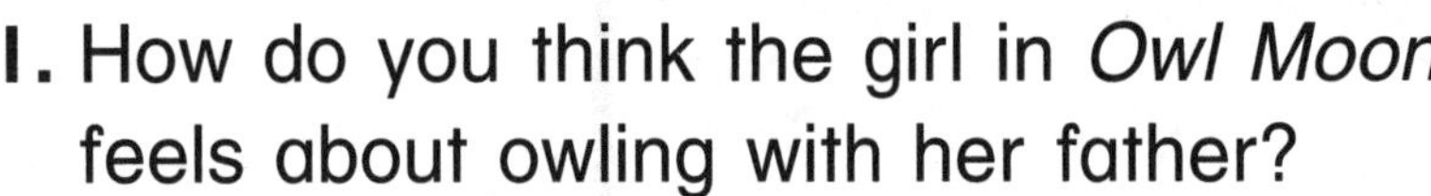

1. How do you think the girl in *Owl Moon* feels about owling with her father?

2. Do you think the person who wrote this book report would read another book by Jane Yolen? Why or why not?

Discuss whether Jane Yolen had to know facts about owls to write *Owl Moon*. Why do you think so?

Name ______________________________

Spell, Write, and Tell

Say, spell, and talk about each word in the box. Then write six pairs of homonyms.

new
blew
sale
too
for
to
sail
night
knew
knight
blue
four

1	2	3
4	5	6

Write a poem about summer. Use one or more of your spelling words. Then share your poem with the class.

new	blew	sale	too	for	to
sail	night	knew	knight	blue	four

LESSON 124: Connecting Spelling, Writing, and Speaking

PHONICS Alive at Home

With your child, use the words in the box to write a poem about something you did together outside.

Name ______________________________

Look and Learn

Let's read and talk about Grand Canyon National Park.

It's the biggest. It's the oldest. It's the most unusual. It's Grand Canyon National Park, and it's filled with things to do. You can take a tour bus. You can take a boat. If you're twelve years old, you can ride a mule. You can choose a trail and go for a hike. But don't go too far. Remember that anyone who goes down has to climb back up!

Think about hiking down into the Grand Canyon. What would you like most? What would you like least?

Circle the word in each list that means the **same** or **nearly the same** as the word in **bold** print.

1 **run**	2 **big**	3 **glad**	4 **shout**
walk	small	sleepy	yell
legs	large	happy	whisper
jog	thin	sad	talk
5 **begin**	6 **rush**	7 **noise**	8 **quick**
write	soon	hear	slow
start	go	quiet	fast
end	hurry	sound	still

Circle two words in each row that have **opposite** meanings.

9.	stop	look	car	go
10.	door	front	back	open
11.	smooth	clean	garden	dirty
12.	in	out	last	next
13.	left	new	quiet	right
14.	below	lost	found	weak

Circle two words in each box that **sound the same** but have different spellings and meanings.

15		16		17	
mad	made	knot	not	reed	ride
mud	maid	note	knit	road	rode
18		**19**		**20**	
door	dear	blew	blend	tall	tail
deer	do	blind	blue	tell	tale

PHONICS Alive at Home Review this Check-Up with your child.

Name ______________________________ Year 20___ – 20___

STUDENT SKILLS ASSESSMENT CHECKLIST

◪ Assessed ☒ Retaught ■ Mastered

Unit 1 Initial, Final, and Medial Consonants

- ❑ Initial Consonants
- ❑ Final Consonants
- ❑ Medial Consonants

Unit 2 Short Vowels

- ❑ Short Vowel **a**
- ❑ Short Vowel **i**
- ❑ Short Vowel **o**
- ❑ Short Vowel **u**
- ❑ Short Vowel **e**
- ❑ High-Frequency Words **around, because, does, right, wash, why**

Unit 3 Long Vowels

- ❑ Long Vowel **a**
- ❑ Long Vowel **i**
- ❑ Long Vowel **o**
- ❑ Long Vowel **u**
- ❑ Long Vowel **e**
- ❑ High-Frequency Words **don't, found, green, its, sing, use**

Unit 4 Variant Consonant Sounds and Consonant Blends

- ❑ Hard and Soft **c**
- ❑ Hard and Soft **g**
- ❑ Initial **l**-blends
- ❑ Initial **r**-blends
- ❑ Initial **s**-blends
- ❑ Final Consonant Blends
- ❑ High-Frequency Words **always, best, buy, their, us, work**

Unit 5 Syllables, Compound Words, y as a Vowel, Consonant Digraphs, and r-controlled Vowels

- ❑ Two-Syllable Words
- ❑ Compound Words
- ❑ **y** as a Vowel
- ❑ Words Ending in **le**
- ❑ Initial Consonant Digraphs **th, sh, wh, ch**
- ❑ Final Consonant Digraphs **ck, th, sh, ch**
- ❑ Consonant Digraph **kn**
- ❑ Consonant Digraph **wr**
- ❑ **ar**-words
- ❑ **or**-words
- ❑ **er**-words, **ir**-words, **ur**-words
- ❑ High-Frequency Words **first, or, very, which, would, your**

Teacher Comments

Unit 6

Vowel Digraphs and Diphthongs

- ❑ Vowel Digraph **ea**
- ❑ Vowel Digraph **oo**
- ❑ Vowel Digraphs **au** and **aw**
- ❑ Diphthongs **ow** and **ou**
- ❑ Diphthongs **oi, oy, ew**
- ❑ High-Frequency Words **before, both, fast, off, sleep, wish**

Unit 7

Contractions, Plurals, and Inflectional Endings

- ❑ Contractions with **not**
- ❑ Contractions with **will**
- ❑ Contractions with **am, is, are**
- ❑ Contractions with **have, has, us**
- ❑ Plural Endings **s** and **es**
- ❑ Changing **y** to **i** Before Adding Plural Ending **es**
- ❑ Inflectional Endings **s** and **es**
- ❑ Inflectional Ending **ing**
- ❑ Inflectional Ending **ed**
- ❑ Changing **y** to **i** Before Adding Inflectional Ending **es** or **ed**
- ❑ Dropping Final **e** Before Adding **ing** or **ed**
- ❑ Doubling Final Consonant Before Adding **ing** or **ed**
- ❑ High-Frequency Words **call, many, read, those, upon, write**

Unit 8

Suffixes, Prefixes, Synonyms, Antonyms, and Homonyms

- ❑ Suffix **ful**
- ❑ Suffixes **less** and **ness**
- ❑ Suffix **ly**
- ❑ Suffixes **er** and **est**
- ❑ Spelling Changes Before Adding **er** and **est**
- ❑ Prefix **re**
- ❑ Prefix **un**
- ❑ Prefix **dis**
- ❑ Synonyms
- ❑ Antonyms
- ❑ Homonyms
- ❑ High-Frequency Words **been, cold, five, goes, pull, these**

Teacher Comments

Think about your best friend and what you like to do together. Then draw a picture.

8

Name ________

Friends of Mine

Reading at Home: Read the book with your child. Talk about what the friends do together in the story. Then have your child identify consonant sounds in words in the story.

1

Directions: Cut and fold the book.

Carmela is my friend.
We play soccer together.
2
Jared is my brother.
He is my best friend.
7
Fold
Hector is my reading partner.
We read good books together.
4
Megan is my neighbor.
We listen to music and dance.
5
Fold

Directions: Cut and fold the book.

Rivers cutting through the land,
2
Fold
Water pumped
from farmers' wells.
7
Raindrops falling on city blocks,
4
Fold
Waves crashing
around the rocks.
5

Name ______________________

Reading at Home: Read the book with your child to find out about different kinds of leaves and seeds. Have your child find words with long vowels, such as **trees, oak, pine, blue,** and **name.**

1

Fold

Pine trees and blue spruce have needles for leaves. They keep their leaves all year.

3

Some seeds are inside fruit.
Can you describe the seed of an apple, an orange, a lime, or a peach?

6

Draw a picture of a leaf or a seed.
Write its name.

8

Directions: Cut and fold the book.

There are many different trees.
Each kind of tree has a different leaf.

2

Some seeds are nuts. Walnuts, pecans, almonds, and Brazil nuts are all seeds.

7

Fold

Some trees, like oaks and maples, lose their leaves in the fall. New leaves grow back in the spring.

4

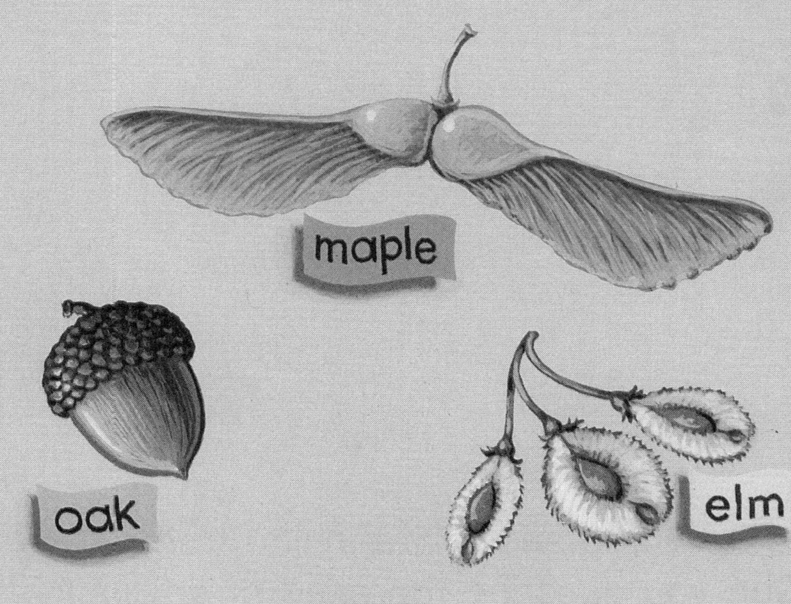

Trees grow from seeds.

5

Fold

Reading at Home: After reading the book with your child, ask if the city is "the best." Why or why not? Together, find a word that begins with a consonant blend, such as **trucks,** and a word with a soft **c** or soft **g,** such as **city** or **giant.**

1

Cars and trucks are slow or fast,
Blocks of people move right past.
Slow—fast—move right past.

3

Lights are blinking, high and low,
Red means stop, green means go.
Red—green—stop and go.

6

Uptown, downtown, children say,
It's the place to work and play.
Uptown—downtown—work and play.

8

Directions: Cut and fold the book.

EAST SIDE
WEST SIDE
Boys and girls from east and west
Think the city is the best.
East—west—city's best.
2
Music, dancing, friends to meet,
Spinning feet step to the beat.
Sing—dance—to the beat.
7
Giant buildings made of brick,
Elevators go up quick.
Up—down—make it quick!
4
7th AV.
88
Under streets, down below,
Trains with folks go to and fro.
Trains—folks—to and fro.
5
Fold
Fold

Magic Carpet Ride

Name ______________

Reading at Home: After reading the book together, ask your child to retell the story. Then look for words with the letters **th, sh, wh, ch, ck, wr,** or **kn.** Also look for compound words, such as **inside** or **anywhere.**

1

Fold

Inside the trunk under some shirts was a purple carpet. The note on the carpet said, "I will take you anywhere you wish to go."

3

Fold

If you had a magic carpet, where would you go? Draw a picture and write about it.

8

Then the children visited China. They saw a furry panda eating bamboo.

6

Directions: Cut and fold the book.

One rainy afternoon, Theo and Barb went up to the attic to explore. They found a big blue trunk in the corner.

2

"I've always wanted to see a real rain forest," said Barb. So they went to Brazil and saw thousands of trees and other plants along the Amazon River.

7

"Let's go to the Rocky Mountains," said Theo. With a swish, they began to fly over the treetops. They landed on a beautiful mountaintop.

4

Next they went to Tanzania. They saw giraffes, elephants, and lions. "I didn't know that giraffes were so tall," said Barb.

5

Blue is the sea where fish swim around,
Moving so smoothly without a sound.

8

Fold

Name ______________

Reading at Home: Read the book with your child. Talk about the different kinds of things pictured and their colors. Together, find words with the letters **ea, oo, aw.** Also look for words with the letters **ow, ou, oi, ew.**

1

Brown is a deer with her spotted fawn.

6

Fold

White is snow that covers the street.

3

Directions: Cut and fold the book.

Red is a strawberry, both juicy and sweet.

2

Green is a meadow moist with dew.

4

Fold

Orange is the pumpkin whose face I drew.

5

Yellow is the sun that we see at dawn.

7

Fold

Name ______________________

Reading at Home: Read the book with your child and answer the questions. Have your child find the plural for **peach (peaches)** and **apple (apples).** Then look for contractions, such as **let's,** and a word that ends with **ing (shopping).**

1

3

There's a sale on juice boxes. "Let's see," Milo says. "I'll get one box for Sara and one for Tara, one for Moe and one for Joe. Oh, and I can't forget me!" Juice boxes come 6 to a pack. Does Milo need more than one pack?

yes no

6

no

Milo pays for his groceries. The cashier says, "Here's 29 cents change." Which coins should Milo get?

Thanks for helping Milo!

8

2 dimes, 1 nickel, 4 pennies

Fold

Fold

Directions: Cut and fold the book.

Let's help Milo with his shopping.
Circle the best answer to each question.

Milo says, "I'll start with fruit." One pound of peaches costs $1.00. Milo gets 3 pounds. How much will he spend on peaches?

$1.00 $3.00 $8.00

$3.00

Fold

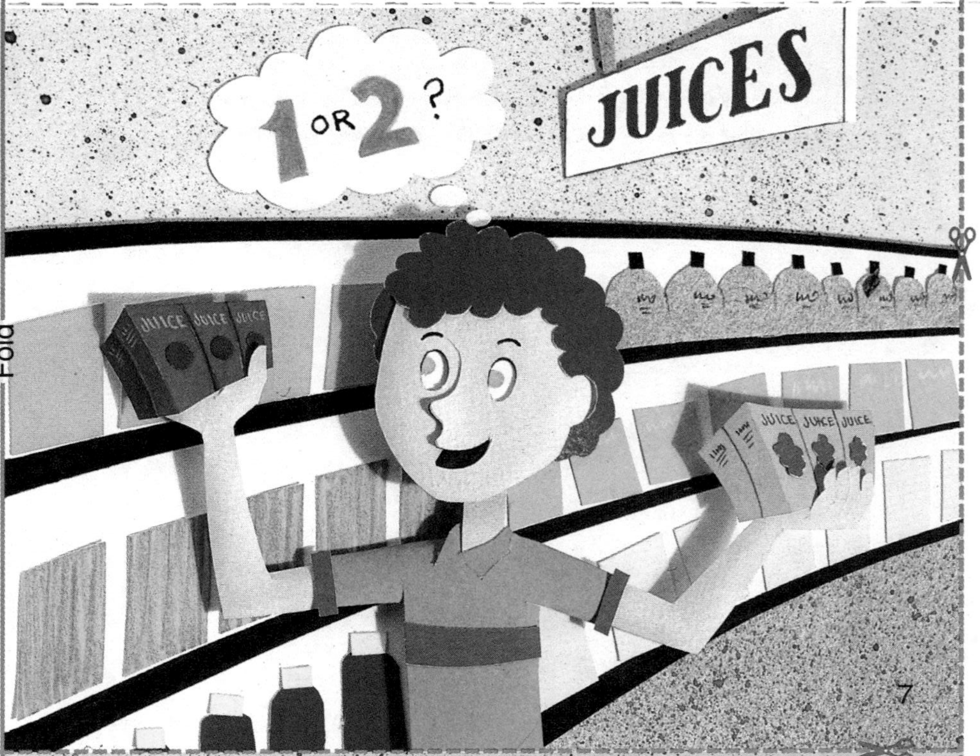

Milo thinks, "An apple a day keeps the doctor away. Maybe I'll eat an apple every day next week." How many apples should Milo buy for next week?

1 apple 7 apples 12 apples

7 apples

Fold

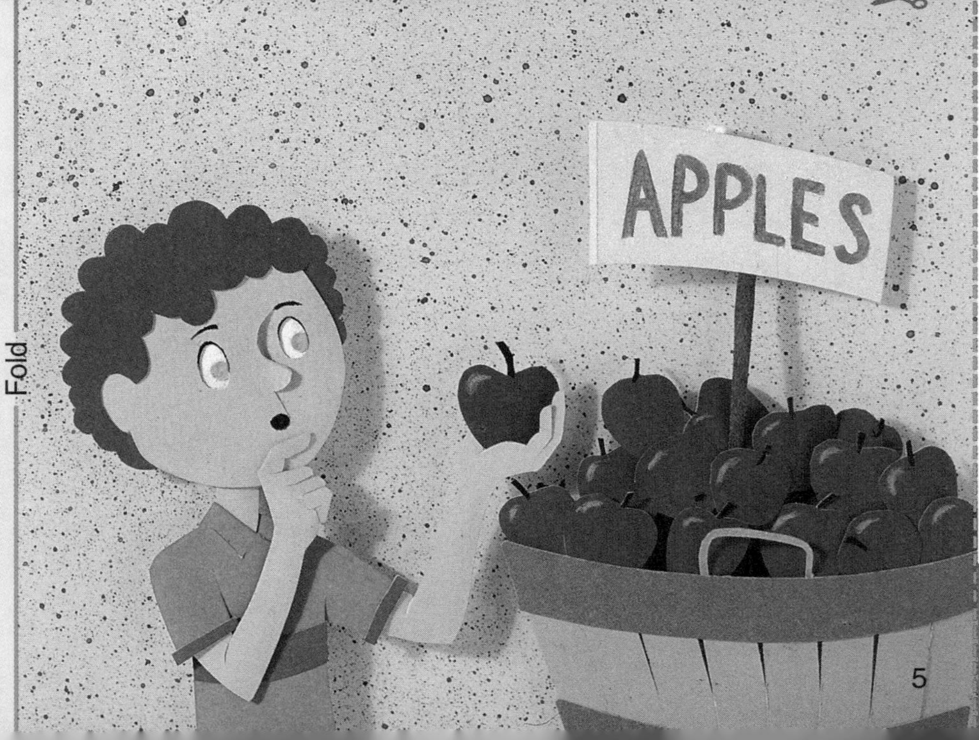

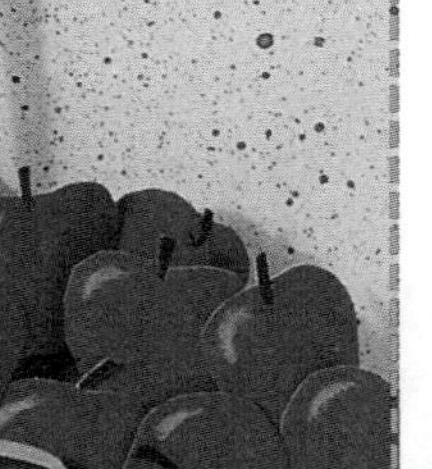

That night, the colorful lights were like twinkling stars.

8

Fold

Name ____________________

A WONDERFUL DAY

Reading at Home: After reading the book with your child, ask where the story takes place. Help your child find a word with a suffix, a word with a prefix, a synonym for **great (wonderful),** an antonym for **full (empty),** and a homonym for **knight (night).**

Then we got into an empty seat at the bottom of the Ferris wheel. As we rode to the top, we could see the cars and the road below us. This was the tallest ride I've ever been on. It was taller than my apartment building!

6

Fold

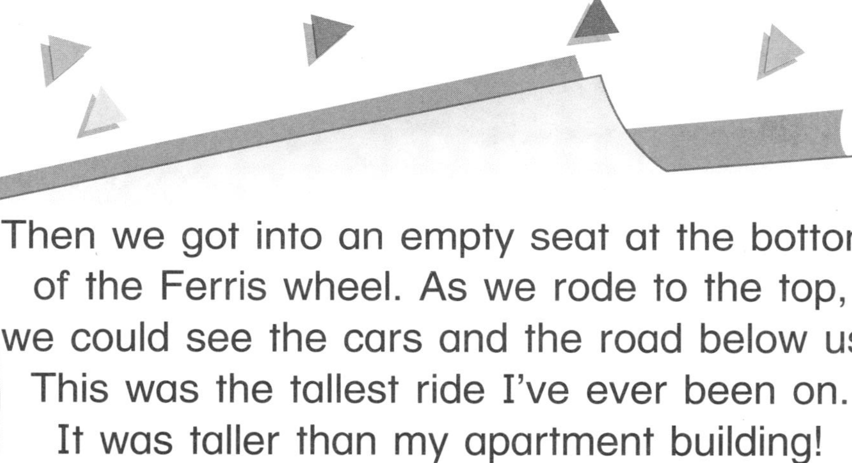

3

Directions: Cut and fold the book.

Last summer, my family went to the biggest amusement park I've ever seen. There were hundreds of families there.

First we went on the merry-go-round. The music played loudly as our horses moved up and down.

2

Fold

7

Next we rode on an unusual roller coaster. The cars went upside down around a huge loop. I was thankful when that ride ended!

4

Fold

5